Strategic Plan for Federal Research and Monitoring of Ocean Acidification

Prepared by
Interagency Working Group on Ocean Acidification
Subcommittee on Ocean Science and Technology
Committee on Environment, Natural Resources, and Sustainability
National Science and Technology Council

Report directed by Section 12404(c) and guided by Section 12405 of the Federal Ocean Acidification Research and Monitoring Act of 2009
(FOARAM Act)

INTERAGENCY WORKING GROUP ON OCEAN ACIDIFICATION MEMBERS

National Oceanic and Atmospheric Administration
Elizabeth Jewett*, Chair
Ned Cyr
Richard Feely
Kenric Osgood
Christopher Sabine
Krisa Arzayus
Steve Gittings

National Science Foundation
David Garrison*, Vice-chair

Bureau of Ocean Energy Management, (BOEM)
Jennifer Culbertson*

Department of State
Kenli Kim*

Environmental Protection Agency
Jason Grear*
Christopher Moore

National Aeronautics and Space Administration (NASA)
Paula Bontempi*, Vice-chair
Kathy Tedesco

U.S. Fish and Wildlife Service (FWS)
Bret Wolfe*

U.S. Geological Survey (USGS)
Lisa Robbins*
Kimberly Yates

U.S. Navy
Justine Kimball*

U.S. Department of Agriculture
Maxwell H. Mayeaux*

The Interagency Working Group on Ocean Acidification (IWG-OA) acknowledges past members: Mary Boatman (BOEM), Phillip Taylor and Priscilla Viana (formerly with NSF), Todd Capson (formerly with DOS), Katherine Nixon (formerly with U.S. Navy) and Fredric Lipshultz (formerly with NASA), for their contributions to early drafts of the Plan, as well as Gayle Pugh (NSF) for providing substantial editorial input. Carlos Del Castillo (NASA), Mark Fornwall (USGS), and Steven Hankin (NOAA) also contributed to revisions of the Plan. Erin Seney and Jennifer Howard (formerly NOAA) oversaw compilation and revision of the document. Courtney Barry (NOAA) contributed design and layout of the document.

* Lead member from each agency. Members listed as of March 2014.

Dear Partners and Friends in our ocean and coastal community,

Oceans provide vital resources and services for sustaining humankind including food, recreation, transportation, energy, nutrient cycling and climate moderation, and they substantially contribute to our economy. However, the chemistry of the oceans is changing in ways that will have impacts on these services and resources far into the future.

Recognizing the need for a comprehensive interagency plan to address the increasing impacts of ocean acidification, Congress passed the Federal Ocean Acidification Research and Monitoring Act of 2009 (FOARAM Act), which defines ocean acidification as "the decrease in pH of the Earth's oceans and changes in ocean chemistry caused by chemical inputs from the atmosphere, including carbon dioxide." Coastal and estuarine acidification, to the extent that the cause of the acidification can be traced back to anthropogenic atmospheric inputs to the ocean, are assumed to be covered by this Strategic Plan for Federal Research and Monitoring of Ocean Acidification (Strategic Plan) wherever ocean acidification is referenced.

The FOARAM Act called for the Subcommittee on Ocean Science and Technology (SOST) to establish an Interagency Working Group on Ocean Acidification (IWG-OA). The Act also explicitly called for developing a strategic research plan to guide "Federal research and monitoring on ocean acidification that will provide for an assessment of the impacts of ocean acidification on marine organisms and marine ecosystems and the development of adaption and mitigation strategies to conserve marine organisms and marine ecosystems." Per requirements of the FOARAM, the original draft plan was open for public comment for two months and also was reviewed by the National Research Council. Edits to this plan were made to address comments that were received. Details about editing decisions are available upon request.

The IWG-OA was chartered in October 2009. These agencies have come together to provide a thoughtful, strategic approach to understand and address the rapidly emerging problem of ocean acidification. This plan is essential to guide federal ocean acidification investments and activities over the next decade and beyond. It will provide a better understanding of the process of ocean acidification, its effects on marine ecosystems, and the steps that must be taken to minimize harm from ocean acidification.

We organized the plan around the following seven priority areas 1) research, 2) monitoring, 3) modeling, 4) technology development, 5) socioeconomic impacts, 6) education and outreach and 7) data management. This plan is the result of a collaborative, thoughtful, and dedicated effort by a large number of people. My thanks goes out to all who contributed to this plan.

Sincerely,

Elizabeth Jewett
Chair of the IWG-OA

Ned Cyr
Former Chair of the IWG-OA

Table of Contents

Executive Summary

Oceans provide vital resources and services for sustaining humankind including food, recreation, transportation, energy, nutrient-cycling, and climate moderation, and they substantially contribute to the economy. However, the chemistry of the oceans is changing in ways that will have impacts on these services and resources. Several federal agencies are working towards developing a collective approach to understand and address this rapidly emerging problem, commonly referred to as ocean acidification. Recognizing the need for a comprehensive interagency plan to address the increasing impacts of ocean acidification, Congress passed the Federal Ocean Acidification Research and Monitoring Act of 2009 (FOARAM Act), which defines ocean acidification as "the decrease in pH of the Earth's oceans and changes in ocean chemistry caused by chemical inputs from the atmosphere, including carbon dioxide." Coastal and estuarine acidification, to the extent that the cause of the acidification can be traced back to anthropogenic atmospheric inputs to the ocean, are assumed to be covered by this Strategic Plan for Federal Research and Monitoring of Ocean Acidification (Strategic Plan) wherever ocean acidification is referenced. To further clarify, anthropogenic effects on land-based runoff can drive respiration-induced acidification that likely exacerbates chemical changes caused by atmospheric CO_2 loading.

The FOARAM Act calls on the Subcommittee on Ocean Science and Technology (SOST) to establish an Interagency Working Group on Ocean Acidification (IWG-OA). The Act also explicitly calls for developing a strategic research plan to guide "Federal research and monitoring on ocean acidification that will provide for an assessment of the impacts of ocean acidification on marine organisms and marine ecosystems and the development of adaption and mitigation strategies to conserve marine organisms and marine ecosystems." The IWG-OA was chartered in October 2009 and comprises representatives from the National Oceanic and Atmospheric Administration (NOAA), National Science Foundation (NSF), Bureau of Ocean Energy Management (BOEM), U.S. Department of State (DOS), U.S. Environmental Protection Agency (EPA), U.S. Fish and Wildlife Service (FWS), National Aeronautics and Space Administration (NASA), U.S. Department of Agriculture (USDA), U.S. Geological Survey (USGS), and the U.S. Navy. The IWG-OA is chaired by NOAA and co-vice chaired by NSF and NASA.

The IWG-OA is guided by the following vision: "**A nation, globally engaged and guided by science, sustaining healthy marine and coastal ecosystems, communities, and economies through informed responses to ocean acidification.**" This vision reflects the intention that U.S. ocean-acidification efforts be societally relevant and to be based on the best available information and science.

In preparing this Strategic Plan, the IWG-OA focused on seven priority themes identified in the FOARAM Act. The themes include the five Program Elements set forth as the minimum requirements for the plan and two additional elements required for successful implementation. Although activities are separated into themes, most of the work conducted will bridge themes to create a unified whole. Throughout the Strategic Plan, cross-referencing of themes clearly emphasizes these connections. The seven themes address: (1) monitoring; (2) research; (3) modeling; (4) technology development; (5) socioeconomic impacts; (6) education, outreach, and engagement strategies; and (7) data management and integration. These themes lay out recommendations and short-term (3- to 5-year) and long-term (10-year) goals.

Research Goals Highlighted

- Improve existing observing systems and develop new technology and systems that monitor chemical and biological impacts of ocean acidification worldwide, document trends, and develop early warning systems.

- Undertake laboratory, mesocosm, and in situ research to examine species-specific and multi-species physiological responses including behavioral and evolutionary adaptive capacities. Also, examine interactions with other stressors, effects on biogeochemical processes affecting the cycling of elements and chemical species, impacts to marine food webs and ecosystems, the ability of ecological processes to reduce ocean acidification or its negative effects, and mechanisms necessary to develop indices to track marine-ecosystem responses.

- Develop comprehensive models to predict changes in the ocean carbon cycle, oceanic carbonate-buffer systems, and impacts on marine ecosystems and organisms.

- Ensure the ability to measure all required parameters with adequate data quality through technology development and standardization of measurements.

- Undertake investigations that translate and reconcile laboratory results with real-world situations.

- Develop vulnerability assessments for various CO_2 emissions scenarios.

- Foster a coordinated Federal approach to technology development and standardization efforts.

- Assess the cultural, subsistence, and economic impacts of ocean acidification.

- Identify and engage stakeholders and local communities in developing adaptation and mitigation strategies for responsible stewardship of marine and Great Lakes organisms and ecosystems.

- Design and coordinate activities that foster ocean-acidification literacy through educational resources and public outreach.

- Develop and implement domestic and international engagement strategies and facilitating partnerships.

- Ensure that results and assessments of monitoring and research efforts are accessible to and understandable by managers, policy makers, and the general public.

- Ensure that ocean-acidification data are properly managed and integrated across disciplinary, organizational, cultural, societal, and data-management technology boundaries.

As ocean-acidification monitoring, research, modeling, and outreach programs are developed, priorities will likely need to be adjusted to ensure coverage of all present and future needs. Allowing for the periodic evaluation and adjustment of the Strategic Plan is a vital part of the planning effort. Areas that are of high interest with respect to ocean acidification in the near-term include high-latitude open-oceans, coral reefs, and coastal and estuarine regions. These regions, and the living marine resources they contain, will receive special emphasis and are incorporated into the short-term and/or long-term goals of each theme.

As ocean acidification is a global phenomenon, international coordination and cooperation is essential. The International Atomic Energy Agency (IAEA) established the Ocean Acidification International Coordination Centre to address the growing concern of ocean acidification. Operated by the Agency's Monaco Environmental Laboratories, the International Coordination Centre will serve the scientific community as well as policymakers, universities, media, and the general public by facilitating, promoting, and communicating global actions on ocean acidification. The United States will be represented on the Ocean Acidification Advisory Board.

The establishment of a National Ocean Acidification Program and an associated National Program Office is recommended to serve the vital role of developing and executing an implementation plan that aligns with the goals outlined in this Strategic Plan. The location and leadership model for the National Ocean Acidification Program Office should be determined by the participating agencies once the National Ocean Acidification Program is confirmed. The National Ocean Acidification Program Office will report directly to the IWG-OA and will be tasked with developing an ocean-acidification implementation plan, coordinating federal and federally funded ocean-acidification research and monitoring, establishing an ocean-acidification information exchange, and producing reports and documentation as required by the FOARAM Act and other statutes and interagency mandates. Both the IWG-OA and National Ocean Acidification Program must ensure that federal ocean acidification monitoring, research, funding programs, and outreach efforts effectively address short- and long-term priorities while remaining proactive and adaptive as ocean acidification impacts and effective mitigation measures become better understood. Also, the National Ocean Acidification Program and Program Office will facilitate U.S. representation on the International Coordination Centre of the IAEA.

Legislative Mandate

The Federal Ocean Acidification Research and Monitoring Act of 2009 (FOARAM Act) directed the Sub-committee on Ocean Science and Technology (SOST) to create an Interagency Working Group on Ocean Acidification (IWG-OA). The IWG-OA was chartered by SOST in October 2009 and includes representatives from the National Oceanic and Atmospheric Administration (NOAA), National Science Foundation (NSF), Bureau of Ocean Energy Management (BOEM), U.S. Department of State (DOS), U.S. Environmental Protection Agency (EPA), National Aeronautics and Space Administration (NASA), U.S. Fish and Wildlife Service (FWS), U.S. Geological Survey (USGS), U.S. Department of Agriculture (USDA), and the U.S. Navy. NOAA chairs the group, and the co-vice chairs are from NSF and NASA. The agencies represented in the IWG-OA have mandates for research and/or management of resources likely to be impacted by ocean acidification (Appendix 1). The group meets regularly to coordinate ocean acidification activities across the Federal government to fulfill the goals of the FOARAM Act.

Section 12404(c) of the FOARAM Act further specifies that the SOST will, not later than 2 years after the date of enactment of the FOARAM Act, transmit a strategic research plan, outlined under section 12405 of the FOARAM Act, to the Committee on Commerce, Science, and Transportation of the Senate and the Committee on Science and Technology and the Committee on Natural Resources of the House of Repre-sentatives. Section 12405 of the FOARAM Act states that "the Subcommittee shall develop a strategic plan for Federal research and monitoring on ocean acidification that will provide for an assessment of the impacts of ocean acidification on marine organisms and marine ecosystems and the development of adaptation and mitigation strategies to conserve marine organisms and marine ecosystems." In addition, the FOARAM Act sets forth the contents, program elements, review, and public participation for the strategic plan.

National Ocean Policy

On July 19, 2010, the President signed an Executive Order establishing the Nation's first comprehensive National Policy for the Stewardship of the Ocean, Our Coasts, and Great Lakes, and adopted the Final Recommendations of the Ocean Policy Task Force (OPTF 2010). The National Ocean Council released the National Ocean Policy Implementation Plan on April 16, 2013 to translate the National Ocean Policy into on-the-ground actions to benefit the American people. The National Ocean Policy Implementation Plan recognizes the importance of addressing ocean acidification in support of coastal and ocean resilience. The development of a strategic research plan for ocean acidification, as requested by the FOARAM Act, is a nec-essary early step towards achieving this National Priority Objective.

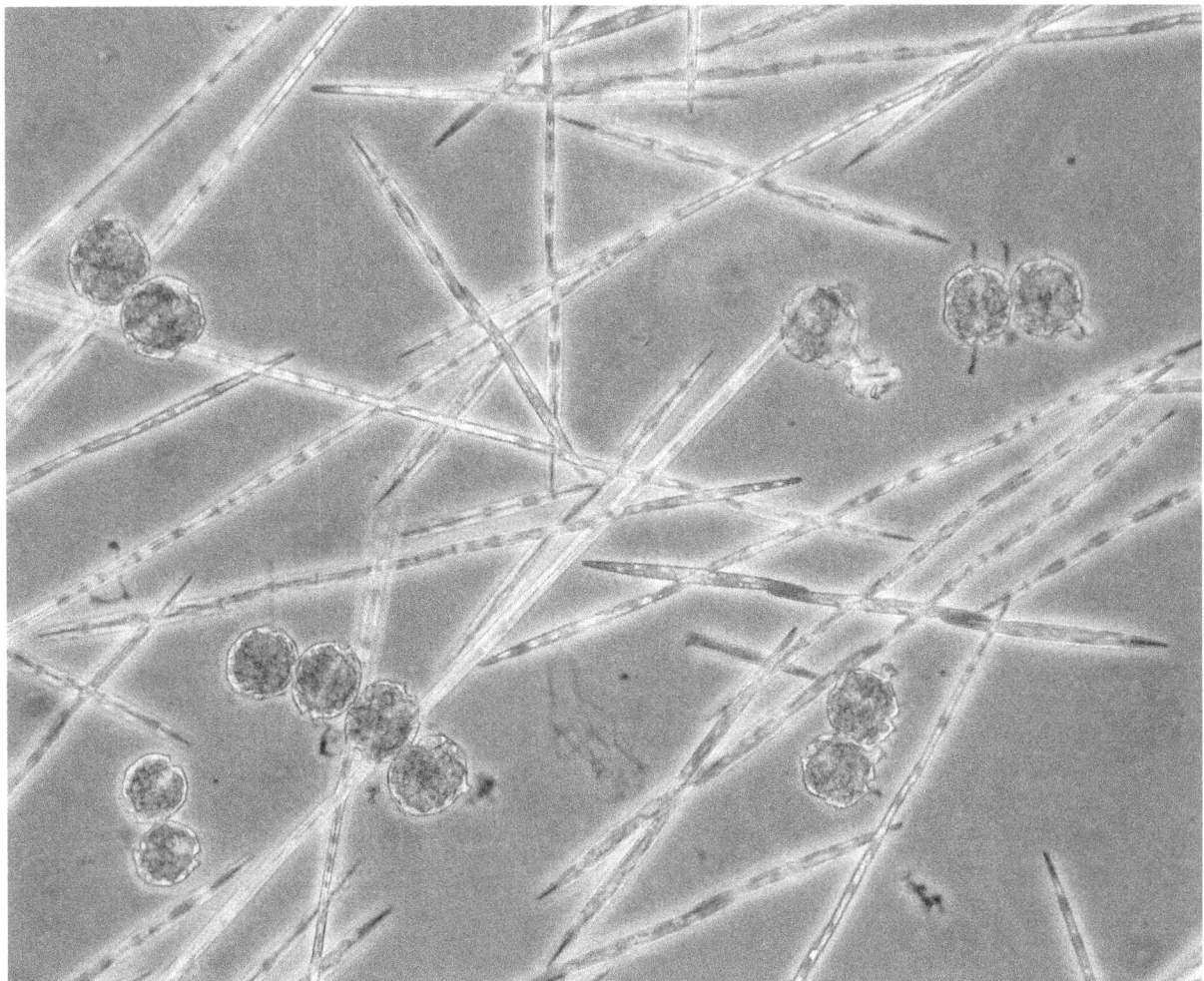

Increasing acidity in the oceans may increase the growth of hamrful algal species such as *Pseudo-nitzschia* and *Alexandrium*, pictured here (Credit: NOAA)

Strategic Plan for Federal Research and Monitoring on Ocean Acidification

Introduction and Background

Human industrial, transportation, and agricultural activities have caused global atmospheric concentrations of carbon dioxide (CO_2) to increase from a pre-industrial average of 280 parts per million (ppm) to the current value of approximately 400 ppm (IPCC AR5 2013). Atmospheric CO_2 concentrations are now higher than experienced on Earth for more than 800,000 years (Lüthi et al. 2008), and the rate of CO_2 release into the atmosphere is likely unprecedented in Earth history (Kump et al. 2009; Hönisch et al. 2012).

Ocean carbonate chemistry is a natural buffering system, but this buffering capacity is being compromised as a direct result of CO_2 absorption by the oceans and to a lesser extent by the absorption of nitric acid (HNO_3) and sulfuric acid ($H2SO4$) at the sea surface (Doney et al. 2007). The oceans have absorbed approximately half of the anthropogenic CO_2 emissions from fossil fuel use and cement manufacturing over the past 200 years (Sabine et al. 2004). This oceanic uptake of CO_2 causes changes to ocean chemistry (Figure 1), including decreases in pH and carbonate ion (CO_3^{2-}) concentrations, collectively known as global ocean acidification (Figure 2). Since the beginning of the industrial revolution, this uptake has caused a lowering of the surface ocean pH globally from about 8.2 to 8.1 (Caldeira and Wickett 2003; Feely et al. 2004; Caldeira and Wickett 2005; Feely et al. 2009), which corresponds to a 26% increase in hydrogen ion concentration, ($H+$, acidity). Reconstruction of past sea surface conditions suggest surface ocean pH has not been this low for at least 2 million years (Hönisch et al. 2009). Orr et al. (2005) predicted an additional decrease in average global ocean surface pH of 0.3 to 0.4 pH units over the 21st century. As a consequence of ocean acidification, the chemistry of the oceans is presently changing at a rate exceeding any known to have occurred for at least the past 20 million years (Feely et al. 2004).

It is not presently known how the changes in seawater chemistry due to ocean acidification will affect marine organisms and ecosystems, though potential responses of some organisms have been examined and, based on current information, changes in marine ecosystems appear to be likely (Raven et al. 2005). Some organisms appear to be particularly sensitive, while others are not (Doney et al. 2009; Ries et al. 2009). Ocean acidification can negatively impact organisms that use calcium carbonate ($CaCO_3$) to build their shells or skeletons (e.g., corals, marine plankton, and shellfish) because it reduces the availability of carbonate ions, which play an important role in shell formation (calcification). Changes in CO_2 and pH can impact other physiological processes as well, affecting species growth, survival, fertilization, embryonic/larval development, and behavior (Fabry et al. 2008; Pörtner 2008; Doney et al. 2009). There will likely be ecological "winners" and "losers" as a result of ocean acidification, causing shifts in the structure and composition of marine food webs and ecosystems.

While our understanding of how ocean acidification affects the range of species driving economic activity, it is clear that the impacts of ocean acidification on marine industry could extend far into and beyond local and regional economies. Ocean acidification also has important cultural implications. To many coastal communities, ocean acidification is a natural resource issue and a significant challenge to their continued cultural identity. For example, many fishers and shellfish farmers depend on shellfish to support their families. Tribal communities also harvest wild and cultured shellfish for ceremonial and subsistence purposes.

Although the FOARAM Act defines ocean acidification as that chemical change attributable to atmospheric inputs, the carbon chemistry of coastal and estuarine waters are influenced by a range of processes in addition to atmospheric input. Local nutrient input from runoff can cause algal blooms (some harmful) and hypoxia. Both primary productivity in surface waters and remineralization of organic matter in deeper waters change the chemistry of the waters influenced. Respiration induced acidification accompanies oxygen drawdown in these nutrient-enriched coastal and estuarine waters. Furthermore, processes driving carbonate mineral production (calcification, precipitation) and loss (bioerosion, dissolution) can also have important localized effects on water chemistry. It is becoming increasingly important to determine the relative contribution of atmospheric CO_2 vs. in-water CO_2 production from respiration, and how much respiration can be traced back to anthropogenic nutrient or organic material input, in an effort to develop effective adaptation strategies.

Vision

The following vision guides the IWG-OA, and consequently the structure and implementation arrangements of the Strategic Plan: "A nation, globally engaged and guided by science, sustaining healthy marine and coastal ecosystems, communities, and economies through informed responses to ocean acidification."

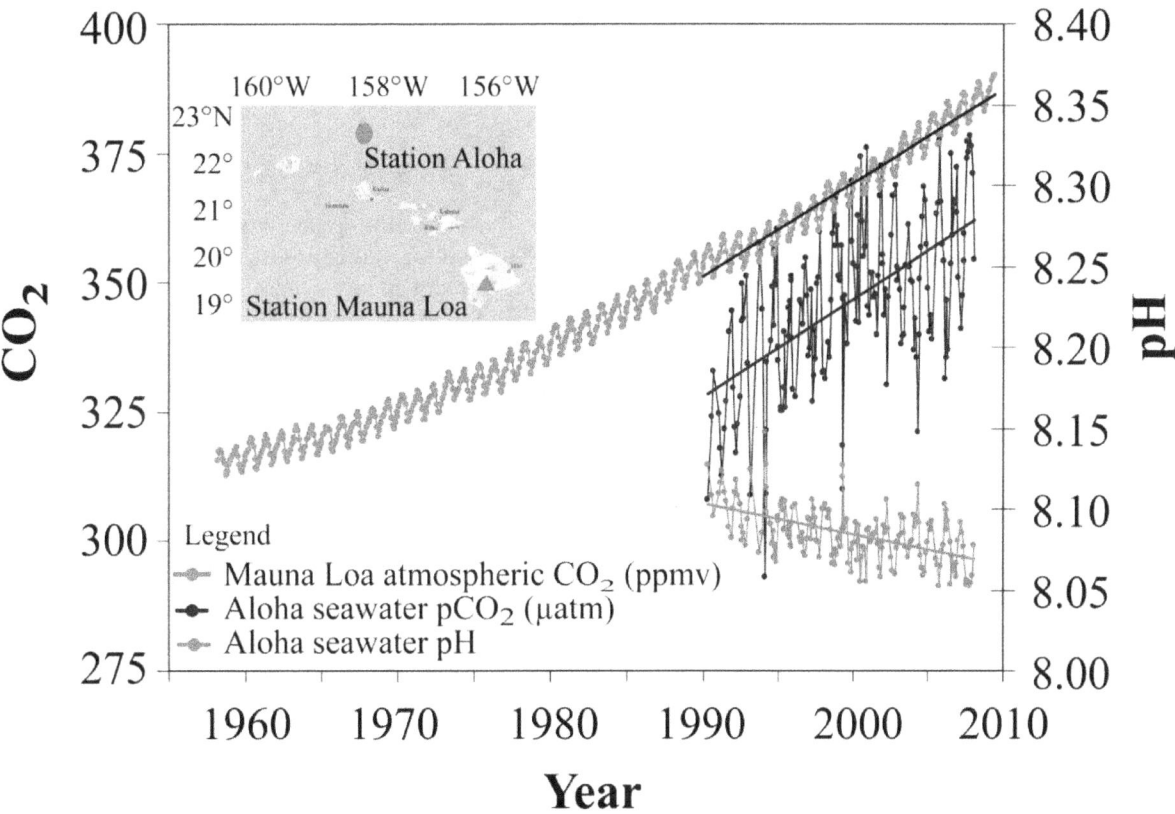

Figure 1. Time-series of atmospheric CO_2 at Mauna Loa, Hawaii (in parts per million volume, ppmv; in red); surface ocean pCO_2 (μatm; in blue); and surface ocean pH (in green) at Ocean Station ALOHA in the subtropical North Pacific Ocean. Note that the increase in oceanic CO_2 over the past 17 years is nearly consistent with the atmospheric increase within the statistical limits of the measurements. Modified after Doney et al. 2009 (Mauna Loa data courtesy of Dr. Pieter Tans, NOAA/Earth System Research Laboratory; Hawaii Ocean Time-Series/ALOHA data courtesy of Dr. David Karl, University of Hawaii; see also Dore et al. 2009).

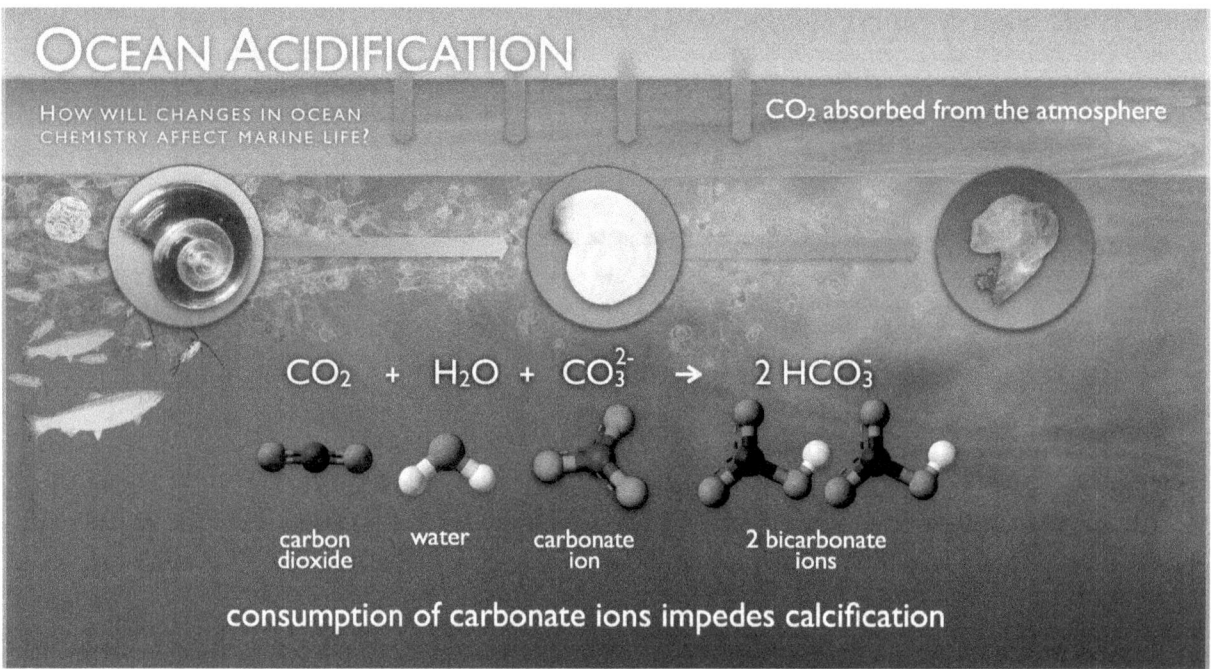

Figure 2. Schematic diagram of ocean acidification processes in the sea (image provided by the NOAA Pacific Marine Environmental Laboratory Carbon Group in collaboration with the University of Washington Center for Environmental Visualization).

Strategic Research Plan

A strategic plan is essential to guide federal ocean acidification investments and activities over the next decade and beyond. Although many Federal agencies currently conduct ocean acidification research and monitoring (Appendix 1), these activities are largely uncoordinated and are not driven by a common vision or purpose. The risk is that agency efforts will be duplicative, or worse, that critical research will not be conducted.

This Strategic Plan presents a clear vision and specific goals to move Federal agencies toward a better understanding of the process of ocean acidification, its effects on marine ecosystems, and the steps that must be taken to minimize harm from ocean acidification. Under this Strategic Plan, the next decade will bring about the implementation of a comprehensive global and regional ocean acidification observing system that includes the monitoring of physical, chemical, biological, social, and cultural effects. Researchers will quantify the effects of ocean acidification under a range of scenarios, time frames, and scales on a wide variety of marine organisms. Enhanced laboratory research, field studies, and modeling efforts will lead to improved understanding of the global and regional biogeochemical processes of ocean acidification and its impact on marine ecosystems and will improve forecasting efforts. A National Ocean Acidification Program will be established to lead U.S. coordination of ocean acidification activities between the Federal agencies, and with academic institutions, industry, and other private sector and international partners. A national ocean acidification data management and information exchange program will ensure that ocean and Great Lakes acidification information reaches scientists, decision makers, and the public in a timely manner. For example, the data and information generated through this Strategic Plan could potentially be used to help States better-address ocean acidification impacts in their marine and Great Lakes coastal waters under various Clean Water Act programs. Finally, the U.S. will join other countries in establishing a robust international research and monitoring program to address what is truly a global challenge. In order to address the complexity of the expected changes, this Strategic Plan is organized into seven priority themes to guide Federal activities in addressing ocean acidification. The themes include the five Program Elements set forth as the minimum requirement mandated in the FOARAM Act and two additional elements inherent to successful implementation of the Strategic Plan:

- Theme 1: "Research to Understand Responses to Ocean Acidification" describes the goals and priorities to understand the physiological responses of marine organisms to ocean acidification and its interactions with other stressors, the impacts to marine food webs, and possible approaches to track ecosystem responses.
- Theme 2: "Monitoring of Ocean Chemistry and Biological Impacts" identifies sampling programs that collect ocean acidification relevant data and prioritizes additional monitoring systems necessary for adequate data collection and monitoring.
- Theme 3: "Modeling to Predict Changes in the Ocean Carbon Cycle and Impacts on Marine Ecosystems and Organisms" summarizes requirements and recommendations for modeling ocean acidification, and its impacts on marine organisms and ecosystems, including codifying our research understanding and studying the interplay of factors affecting marine ecosystems, thus permitting analysis of the efficacy of adaptation and mitigation strategies.
- Theme 4: "Technology Development and Standardization of Measurements" describes goals that improve the ability to measure all required parameters through technology development and adequate data quality via measurement standardization.
- Theme 5: "Assessment of Socioeconomic Impacts and Development of Strategies to Conserve Marine Organisms and Ecosystems" focuses on assessing the economic and cultural impacts of ocean acidification and developing adaptation and mitigation strategies.
- Theme 6: "Education, Outreach, and Engagement Strategy on Ocean Acidification" describes goals for designing and coordinating educational, public outreach, and domestic and international engagement activities, as well as ensuring results and assessments of monitoring and research efforts are accessible to and understandable by all stakeholders.
- Theme 7: "Data Management and Integration" discusses the need for effective data management and integration within the context of other international, Federal, State, local, and private activities.

Integration of these themes is essential to the success of the Strategic Plan and for timely responses to real-world issues (see Box 1). For example, there needs to be dynamic and iterative linkage between modeling, research, and observation. Also, socioeconomic research and the ability of that work to inform adaptive policy responses depends upon both predictive ecosystem modeling and, in the long term, monitoring of system responses to those adaptive policy changes. All themes need to be underpinned by data management and education. It is intended for the Strategic Plan to be implemented in a coordinated and integrated manner that provides for the flow of new information and developments between the various science communities and other stakeholders. This integration will be further detailed in the Implementation Plan.

Freshly harvested oysters from Yaquina Bay, Oregon (Credit: NOAA)

Box 1. Ocean Acidification: From Knowledge to Action, Washington State's Strategic Response.

Beginning in 2007, oyster hatcheries along the Oregon and Washington State coasts began experiencing massive mortalities of the young larvae. It took several years, and near disaster, to figure out that the cause was the upwelling of corrosive water which was being taken into the hatcheries during crucial hatching and growing periods. The hatchery scientists tried several interventions before seeking the advice of carbon scientists, like Burke Hales (OSU) and Richard Feely (NOAA), to ask the question whether changes in the carbon chemistry might be driving the failures. Through the assistance of these scientists (Barton *et al* 2012), the hatcheries were able to install observing systems and institute adaptation measures which brought the hatchery industry back from the brink of failure.

credit: NOAA

Governor Christine Gregoire of Washington State, in an effort to address the growing oyster hatchery and wild set crisis, created a Blue Ribbon Panel on Ocean Acidification. The panel convened scientists, state, and federal government officials, non-governmental organizations, state legislators, shellfish industry scientists, owners, and prominent citizens. This interdisciplinary, coordinated process led to sound scientific findings and recommendations which the Governor then moved forward with a signed Executive Order in November 2012. The Executive Order requested a very interdisciplinary, interagency approach to addressing ocean acidification impacts in Washington State and may serve as a model for other states and multi-state actions.

The Oregon and Washington State oyster crisis is an excellent real-world example where knowledge of species biology (Theme 1) and observations (Theme 2) were able to inform not only policy and management practices, but also the public about the risks associated with acidified ocean waters (Theme 6 and 7) and how that information was utilized to assist crucial local economies (Theme 5) and predict future events (Theme 3 and 4).

Priorities and Metrics

The FOARAM Act requires the National Ocean Acidification Program to provide biennial progress reports and a revised 10-year plan every 5 years. This requirement dictates that progress of the various elements of the program be evaluated. To this end, it is important that metrics be established to measure progress towards the Strategic Plan's goals, and that these evaluations of the program be used to set priorities in an iterative fashion. The research and monitoring goals in the Strategic Plan are divided into short-term and long-term goals for each Theme.

Initial priorities and metrics prescribed in the FOARAM Act (see Legislative Mandate) are responsibilities of the IWG-OA (also see below). These include developing the present Strategic Plan, establishing a National Program Office, and developing an Implementation Plan. Agency budgets and opportunities will determine the priorities for implementation across the seven themes outlined in this Strategic Plan. In crafting the Implementation Plan and outlining specific actions and programs, specific performance metrics will be developed for each activity as appropriate. The National Academy report, "Thinking Strategically: The Appropriate Use of Metrics for the Climate Change Science Program"(NRC 2005), provides guidance appropriate for establishing evaluation metrics for ocean acidification research and monitoring activities. It is expected that appropriate evaluation metrics for specific agency-supported activities will develop as part of an Implementation Plan. The National Program Office will be charged with developing overall evaluation metrics for the program that incorporate and integrate the performance metrics for specific actions or programs. Performance metrics will be used in conjunction with ad hoc peer review, periodic evaluation by external advisory panels and community-planning workshops as needed to evaluate and direct the ocean acidification research and monitoring program. Setting priorities, goals, and developing metrics for activities outlined in the Strategic Plan are likely to be an incremental process and will be determined largely by federal budget priorities.

Research and monitoring activities focused on ocean acidification have begun and are addressing many of the short-term goals outlined in the Strategic Plan. Priorities for present activities are determined by:

- The FOARAM Act: The Act specifies actions by the IWG-OA and requires biennial reporting from participating agencies. Metrics required by the FOARAM Act will be incorporated in future metric and evaluation criteria.
- National Ocean Policy Implementation Plan: Ocean acidification is mentioned throughout this document and several agencies have committed to action items that address ocean acidification and related issues such as carbon sequestration.
- Ongoing high priority research areas by participating agencies: For example, NSF's Science, Engineering and Education for Sustainability (SEES) program supports research funding that covers several themes in the Strategic Plan.
- Existing agency research plans: Many agencies have research plans that include some activities related to ocean acidification that can provide guidance on priority development. For example, NOAA's Ocean and Great Lakes Acidification Research Plan and the Interagency Ocean Acidification Data Management Plan.
- Community input from Ocean Carbon and Biogeochemistry (OCB) program office: The Ocean Acidification Subcommittee of OCB hosts annual Principal Investigator meetings, supports training activates, and supports community building workshops on topics related to carbon cycling and ocean acidification. OCB activities provide timely information to the agencies about the progress of ocean acidification research including gaps in research areas and emerging opportunities. OCB also provides an umbrella for U.S. representation in several international organizations. OCB is particularly well-positioned to facilitate international ocean acidification activities.

Relationship to Previous Efforts

This strategic plan builds upon numerous reports and studies that have been supported over the recent past by U.S. Federal agencies and other entities. Some of the major reports considered are:

- Intergovernmental Panel on Climate Change (IPCC) Workshop on Impacts of Ocean Acidification on Marine Biology and Ecosystems (IPCC 2011). This workshop report provides syntheses of these perspectives for the workshop's core topics: the changing chemistry of the oceans, impacts of ocean acidification for individual organisms, and scaling-up responses from individual organisms to ecosystem levels.
- 2010 National Research Council (NRC) report, Ocean Acidification: A National Strategy to Meet the Challenges of a Changing Ocean (NRC 2010a). This report is a review of the state of knowledge and identifies key gaps in information to help Federal agencies develop a National Ocean Acidification Program that will improve understanding and address the consequences of ocean acidification.
- Community White Papers for OceanObs'09: Sustained Ocean Observations and Information for Society (Hall *et al.* 2010 and papers therein). White papers describe observing systems, sensors, and data management critical to an ocean acidification program.
- *Report on Research Priorities for Ocean Acidification* (Orr *et al.* 2009). This report resulted from the Second Symposium on the "Ocean in a High-CO_2 World" held in 2008, which provided an interdisciplinary forum to assess what is known about ocean acidification and priorities for future research.
- 2008 Report of the Ocean Carbon and Biogeochemistry Scoping Workshop on Ocean Acidification Research, *Present and Future Impacts of Ocean Acidification on Marine Ecosystems and Biogeochemical Cycles* (Fabry *et al.* 2008). This report outlines research activities needed to advance ocean acidification research across four critical ecosystems: high-latitude regions, warm- and cold-water coral reefs, coastal regions including estuaries, and tropical/subtropical pelagic regions.
- *Impacts of Ocean Acidification on Coral Reefs and Other Marine Calcifiers: A Guide for Future Research* (Kleypas *et al.* 2006). This workshop report identifies the most-pressing questions about the effects of rising atmospheric carbon dioxide on marine calcifiers, ecosystems, and the carbon cycle. It also provides guidelines for designing research to address these questions.
- 2005 Royal Society Report, *Ocean Acidification Due to Increasing Atmospheric Carbon Dioxide* (Raven *et al.*

2005). This report provides an overview of the state of scientific knowledge of ocean acidification and its likely impacts on marine organisms.

Establishment of a National Ocean Acidification Program

It is recommended that a National Ocean Acidification Program, and associated National Program Office, be established with oversight by the IWG-OA. The Office should be established outside of the Federal agencies, using the model of the U.S. Joint Global Ocean Flux Study or the Climate Variability and Predictability System (CLIVAR). A major function of the office will be to facilitate coordination between the Federal agencies, the academic community, the public, the international community, and other ocean acidification stakeholders. To support this function, a multi-stakeholder advisory committee will be established.

Functions of the National Program Office will include:

- Develop a detailed Implementation Plan with community input.
- Establish, and support the activities of, a committee that helps identify the rapidly changing needs for research, monitoring, technology development, education, outreach, and other appropriate activities.
- Coordinate and assist with planning of Federal and Federally-funded ocean acidification research and monitoring activities.
- Act as a Federal nexus for State, local, and private-sector partners.
- Coordinate U.S. ocean acidification research and monitoring with international activities;
- Establish an ocean acidification information exchange to provide timely research results and produce syntheses and assessments that will be accessible to and understandable by managers, policy makers, and the general public. The information exchange will serve as a communication avenue between the National Program, scientists, managers, and others seeking decision support.
- Support workshops, advisory group meetings, etc. to develop plans, integrate activities, and communicate issues, activities, and results.
- Develop a comprehensive data management plan in close coordination with ongoing agency efforts.
- Provide input for reports to Congress and other documentation as required by the FOARAM Act and other statutes and interagency mandates.

In the event that an external Program Office cannot be established immediately due to resource constraints, Federal agencies will establish an Interim Program Office within the agencies. The Interim Program Office will maintain the same functions, at a reduced level, as the external Office, but will leverage existing Federal programs so that there are no additional administrative costs. The National Program Office should be supported cooperatively by participating agencies.

Enhancing Coordination between Federal Agencies

Recognizing that the Program Office may not be fully operational in the near future, the member agencies of the IWG-OA will establish interim mechanisms to coordinate their ocean acidification work. Each Theme will stand up an Implementation Team with a designated lead agency. The Teams will be responsible for developing Theme-specific implementation plans, communicating agency activities, highlighting opportunities for coordination, communicating with federal working groups (i.e. the Interagency Working Group on Aquaculture), and engaging with the broader stakeholder community. At least once a year, all Team leads will convene to exchange information and coordinate activities.

Theme 1. Research to Understand Responses to Ocean Acidification

Numerous studies have tested the potential effects of ocean acidification on marine organisms yielding an increasingly complex narrative with a diversity of responses now being documented (Gattuso *et al.* 1998; Kleypas *et al.* 1999; Hoegh-Guldberg *et al.* 2007; Iglesias-Rodriguez *et al.* 2008; Pelejero *et al.* 2010; Waldbusser *et al.* 2011; Nilsson *et al.* 2012). Ocean acidification may threaten whole marine ecosystems and the services they provide. More research is needed to better inform models and improve predictions of: 1) the earth system response to acidification; 2) the impacts of ocean acidification on marine populations and communities; and 3) the capacity of organisms to acclimate or adapt to the changes occurring in response to ocean chemistry. An approach which considers how ocean acidification interacts with other global change-related stresses, such as reduced oxygen and increased temperature, given that exposure to multiple stresses may change the response to any one of them (Pörtner *et al.* 2011), should be emphasized given that ocean acidification is not happening in isolation.

Some of the most significant research challenges are to separate the effects of ocean acidification from other environmental stressors and to estimate the synergistic effects of ocean acidification with other stressors to correctly predict future conditions threatening ecosystems and dependent human communities. In addition, the IPCC (Ocean Acidification workshop, 2011) reported that caution, and considerable thought, must be exercised in applying laboratory findings to real world projections. Little is known about how changing ocean chemistry will affect global ocean biogeochemical cycles of biologically important elements and nutrients and biogeochemical processes such as primary production, respiration, $CaCO_3$ dissolution, bioerosion, redox processes, and nitrogen fixation. A fundamental understanding of the impact of ocean acidification on marine organisms, communities, and ecosystems is needed to develop effective mitigation strategies to increase resilience of economically important organisms, broader ecosystems, and the human communities which rely on them. In addition, biologists studying impacts of current and future ocean acidification on species and ecosystems need to have a more complete understanding of the contemporary water chemistries in which those species naturally reside (informed by Theme 2). This is especially true for coastal and estuarine species which experience large fluctuations in carbonate chemistry in space and time. As findings relevant to managed species and habitats come to light, this information should be closely shared with fishery resource managers and fish culturists for evaluation of future stocks and development of potential adaptation strategies.

Current understanding of ocean acidification impacts on ecosystems has been documented in comprehensive reviews (e.g., Raven *et al.* 2005; Kleypas *et al.* 2006; Fabry *et al.* 2008; Doney *et al.* 2009; NRC 2010a; Gattuso and Hansson 2011). The research needs, recommendations, and goals below focus on major priorities for federally supported research on ocean acidification, and are based mainly on the NRC (2010a), Orr *et al.* (2009), Fabry *et al.* (2008), Workshop on Impacts of Ocean Acidification on Marine Biology and Ecosystems (IPCC 2011), and Royal Society (Raven *et al.* 2005) reports.

Requirements and Recommendations

A successful strategy for ocean acidification research requires special attention to integrated efforts, regionally, nationally, and internationally. Effective management of marine resources in response to ocean acidification will require researchers viewing their contributions in a broader perspective, but there is also clearly a need for research on issues such as vulnerable and economically important species to be conducted at regional scales. To this end, conducting studies on an expanding list of species, rather than focusing resources on in-depth studies of a narrow group of species, should be encouraged although it is also necessary to figure out the physiological mechanisms driving the response as well. Balancing resources between the "expanding list" approach and the in-depth physiological studies will be important. Large facilities and highly interdisciplinary training opportunities will be needed to help scientists succeed in this new field, scale up experiments to the ecosystem level, and develop useful marine and estuarine ecosystem management strategies. Additional investments in technology development will be useful to improve the capability to measure chemical and biological variables over space and time (NRC 2010a).

A solid understanding of the impacts of ocean acidification on marine organisms and ecosystems, including endangered and protected species, is critical to developing early warning systems (Theme 2), predictive models (Theme 3), and indices that will guide adaption and mitigation measures (Theme 5). It will be important to launch efforts simultaneously to gauge which marine species are focal points for human communities (Theme 5) and thus a higher priority for impacts research. Critical research efforts include: understanding species-specific physiological responses and adaptation potential; understanding how effects on organisms will propagate through food webs and ecosystems; developing indices that capture shifts in environmental and ecological responses; and understanding Earth history to inform ocean acidification predictions.

Species-specific Physiological Responses and Adaptation Potential

Biological response of marine organisms to ocean acidification impacts seems to be species-specific, with potential "winners" and "losers" emerging (NRC 2010a). Research has shown calcification rates will decrease for most species (Guinotte and Fabry 2008; Johnson and Carpenter 2012), and that calcification is not the only biological process that is critically influenced by a changing pH and increased CO_2 concentration (Pörtner 2008; Kroeker 2010a, 2013). The biochemical reactions of organisms are profoundly impacted by changes in seawater pH, and unless species can acclimate, avoid, or adapt metabolically, survival and/or reproductive capacity may be compromised.

Understanding the magnitude of these biological changes on ecologically and commercially important organisms is essential to predicting possible impacts of ocean acidification on the structure of marine communities and ultimately on the human communities which rely on them (Theme 5). Similarly, focusing on species important for economic, cultural, or subsistence reasons is key to predicting possible impacts on the industries, cultures, and human communities dependent upon them. Priority should be given to studies taking a "whole-organism" approach that quantifies changes in calcification rates simultaneously with other physiological factors (e.g., changes in metabolism, health, reproductive, and behavioral responses) or, for non-calcifying organisms, "whole organism" studies that address key physiological and life history effects (e.g., fertilization and development) to maximize the probability of detecting ecologically, culturally, and economically important effects and those that may offset effects of ocean acidification (Findlay *et al.* 2009). It is also critical to consider the effect of ocean acidification on all life stages, as species may be insensitive at certain life stages while highly vulnerable during other stages (Kurihara 2008; Talmage and Gobler 2010; Barton *et al.* 2012). After clear positive or negative organism responses to changes in pH or saturation states are identified, species-specific mechanisms that cause those responses should be determined, controlling, if possible, for co-varying factors such as light, flow, temperature, and nutrients. In addition, translation of organismal effects to higher ecological scales (e.g., populations and ecosystems) will require data not typically collected in physiological or organismal studies (see Food Webs and Ecosystems).

Changes to seawater chemistry have been occurring very rapidly on geochemical and evolutionary timescales and there is a justifiable concern as to whether organisms will be able to acclimate or adapt to these changes (NRC 2010a). Research on species acclimation (individual organism adjustment) (Evans and Hofmann 2012; Form and Riebesell 2012), adaptation (population change with time) (Sunday *et al.* 2011, Lohbeck *et al.* 2012), and epigenetic effects (hereditable traits affected by the environment) is necessary to correctly predict future biological response to ocean acidification and the ecosystem impacts. For some organisms, longer term, multi-year studies using realistic CO_2 levels (e.g., those projected for next 100 years) should be emphasized rather than acute effect (very high CO_2 levels) short-term studies (Pörtner 2008). However, short-term acute exposure experiments with increases in magnitude of variability (e.g., pH) may be appropriate for those organisms that experience strong diel-cycling of pH and in coastal systems experiencing increased frequency or severity of upwelling or other acute conditions. Long-term studies which are constructed to look at effects over multiple generations will be critical for examining adaptation mechanisms. Various tools have been developed to evaluate evolutionary mechanisms under ocean acidification and to study the potential for species-specific acclimation and adaptation. These include:
- Controlled laboratory studies;
- Biogeochemical proxy development and paleo-reconstructions;
- Studies located at seafloor vents where high concentrations of CO_2 are emitted to the water column at ambient temperature (Figure 3);

- Studies in regions with naturally high CO_2 levels and/or high variability in carbon chemistry, such as coastal and upwelling systems and the Great Lakes (Lake Superior: Atilla *et al.* 2011);
- Free-Ocean Carbon Enrichment Experiments (FOCE); and
- Genomic and proteomic studies designed to investigate physiological plasticity and adaptive capacity in response to ocean acidification.

Studies investigating the effects of CO_2 on physiological processes should also be conducted in conjunction with those that examine other factors such as temperature, oxygen deficiency, and energy availability because ocean acidification will not be affecting any system in an isolated way. Organisms with sufficient energy supply (i.e., food, nutrients, light, and chemical energy) are likely to be less vulnerable to ocean acidification. Little is known about the simultaneous effects of ocean acidification and warming on physiological processes although a growing number of scientists are now exploring this question (Kleypas and Langdon 2006; Pansch *et al.* 2012; Walther *et al.* 2010). Biological response and changes in marine ecosystems cannot be realistically understood without at least accounting for the effects of climate change simultaneously with elevated seawater partial pressure of CO_2 (pCO_2) and decreased pH. Recent studies have demonstrated the wide-ranging effects of ocean acidification on organismal function, including unanticipated effects on behavior, olfaction, and neurotransmitter action in marine fish (Simpson *et al.* 2011; Briffa *et al.* 2012; Nilsson *et al.* 2012). A widely occurring consequence of ocean acidification involves energy costs involved in regulation of pH values of body fluids (Pörtner *et al.* 2011). In many, if not most animals, costs of pH regulation may rise as ocean pH decreases and these effects are critical to understand. These phenomena are intrinsically coupled as they have the same primary cause: anthropogenic emission of CO_2.

A diverse set of organism types (i.e., different taxa, trophic levels, etc.) must receive attention to achieve robust understanding and predictive capabilities with respect to ecosystem responses, especially those predicted to be most negatively impacted by ocean acidification and those most relied upon for ecosystem services. Groups of organisms that require attention include (Raven *et al.* 2005; Kleypas *et al.* 2006; Joint *et al.* 2010; Garrard *et al.* 2012; Caron and Hutchins 2013):
- Shallow and deep-water corals, especially major reef builders;
- Calcifying and non-calcifying primary producers such as crustose coralline algae, phytoplankton species, sea grasses, and kelp, as well as harmful algal species;
- Calcifying bivalve, crustacean, and echinoderm species which have commercial, ecological, and/or cultural importance;
- Key zooplankton species which provide the critical link between primary production and major commercial fishery species, starting with calcifying species;
- Threatened and endangered species;
- Species with large economic importance such as various vertebrate, molluscan species; and
- Other non-calcifying, ecologically, commercially, or culturally key (and sometimes invasive) species such as fungi, tunicates, jellies, various macroalgae, and microbes which contribute strongly to ecosystem function and process.

Food Webs and Ecosystems

The effects of ocean acidification on specific organisms will propagate through food webs, altering community dynamics, such as predator-prey, commensal, symbiotic, parasitic, and competitive interactions. Research is needed to determine how and where this will happen. Ecosystem models (linked to biogechemical and hydrodynamic models) will be an important tool for forecasting the impact of ocean acidification on ecological communities (Theme 3). These models can also serve as tools to provide insight into which species in the ecosystem are key for the food web and may require heightened attention in laboratory and field studies in an iterative fashion.

Species and ecosystems may acclimate or adapt to ocean acidification and associated changes in primary productivity and nutrient availability but ecosystem roles and functions will change as a result (Fabricius *et al.* 2011; Kroeker *et al.* 2011b). Observations of organismal or physiological responses to stressors are necessary but insufficient to evaluate and predict these changes. For example, the early life stages of two species in a comparative study, may be equally sensitive biologically, but the importance of this biological response to population dynamics and selective pressure for evolutionary adaptation may differ between these two species by orders of magnitude. Such issues have been the traditional domains of life history theory and population demography (e.g., Stearns 1992; Caswell 2001). Better incorporation of such theory into ocean acidification research and in marine science in general will improve linkage and scaling up from physiological and organismal research to food web observations and ecosystem prediction. In addition, application of formal life history theory can facilitate extrapolation of results from "model organisms" to broader taxonomic groups or functional units.

Upper trophic levels may be affected by changes to quantity or composition of the food available and by direct physiological effects (NRC 2010a) (Holcomb *et al.* 2010; Melzner *et al.* 2011). Research that explores how rising ocean temperatures, elevated CO_2, and decreased pH act simultaneously on the distribution of primary producers and then on the higher trophic levels of marine food webs is in its infancy. If decreased biodiversity results from ocean acidification, the stability of ecosystems may be compromised by the possible loss of key trophic linkages and food web integrity and/or an inhibition of ecosystem resilience. Such changes could result in alternative ecosystem states, and ultimately, lead to catastrophic ecosystem changes (NRC 2010a). Vulnerable ecosystems include cold- and warm-water coral reefs (Figure 3); coastal ecosystems subjected to upwelling conditions, especially in the high latitudes; estuaries; and freshwater systems which are more likely to experience multiple stressors and high spatial and temporal variability in seawater temperature, salinity, oxygen, pH, pCO_2, and total alkalinity (TA). Controlled laboratory, mesocosm, and/or field experiments on multi-species assemblages are required to provide the empirical data necessary to grasp the impact of these multiple factors on complex marine ecosystems. Such studies are also required to parameterize mathematical models of ecosystem behavior that will permit examination of interactions with the physical environment and prediction of future states.

Figure 3. Seascapes at: a) control site ('low pCO_2': pH~8.1); b) moderate seeps ('high pCO_2': pH 7.8–8.0); and c) the most intense vents (pH<7.7), showing progressive loss of diversity and structural complexity with increasing pCO_2. d) Map of the main seep site along the western shore of Upa-Upasina. Color contours indicate seawater pH, and the letters indicate the approximate locations of seascapes as shown in a–c. Nature Climate Change, (Fabricius et al. 2011).

Environmental and Ecological Responses and Indices

Key pathways and transformations of ocean carbon and nutrient cycles will likely be affected by ocean acidification. Increased CO_2 and decreased pH in seawater are expected to affect the chemical speciation of nutrients and trace metals (Huesemann *et al.* 2002; Millero *et al.* 2009; Hoffmann *et al.* 2012), which are needed in bioavailable forms for various biochemical processes inside cells. Research suggests the latter will alter phytoplankton abundance and community structure, creating an interactive feedback cycle (Hutchins *et al.* 2009). pH can also affect the toxicity of trace metals and sorption of elements onto natural particles, such as clays, which could have repercussions beyond phytoplankton impacts (Millero *et al.* 2009). Although rates of carbonate sediment dissolution are slow, they will increase as waters become more acidic. On timescales of decades to centuries, $CaCO_3$ dissolution will not significantly counteract ocean acidification, but on timescales of millennia, this process will be the ultimate sink of anthropogenic CO_2 (Archer *et al.* 1998). Nevertheless, as a result of increasing $CaCO_3$ dissolution and increases in bioerosion rates (Tribollet *et al.* 2009), coral reefs could transition from a condition of net accretion to net erosion of $CaCO_3$ (Andersson *et al.* 2009; Silverman *et al.* 2009; Andersson and Gledhill 2013) and some organisms depositing metastable carbonate phases could be faced with the same challenge.

Given the complexity of ecosystems, indices need to be developed that capture their current status and trajectory without having to monitor the status of every component of an ecosystem and yet be confident that the response variables are indicative of an ocean acidification impact. Such indices would be expected to reveal shifts in future states and so aid in the employment of mitigation and adaptation strategies. In an effort to identify these "early warning" indicators, research efforts need to focus on choosing both relevant species and geographic sites (next section, this Theme) for intensive long-term monitoring (see Theme 2). As part of this, we need to design monitoring frameworks for various ecosystems such that response variables can be reasonably traced to changes in the carbonic acid system. Established, well-characterized sites (e.g., Long-Term Ecological Research Program [LTERs], Marine Sanctuaries, ocean time-series locations; refer to Box 2 and 3 for examples) and well-studied species (e.g., pteropods, certain coral species, and sea urchin larvae) will be important for initial efforts; however, these may not be the most-appropriate sites/species for detecting the full impact of ocean acidification. Laboratory dose-response studies and FOCE (in situ controlled experiments) should be integrated with monitored field parameters to identify useful biological indicators of ocean acidification and its effects. Development of the monitoring frameworks will begin as a research effort. Once indices are identified and accepted as bellwether indicators, activities can pass into a monitoring mode.

Understanding Earth History to Inform Ocean Acidification Predictions

The geologic record provides a series of natural experiments that show environmental and biological responses to carbon cycle perturbations of the past. Studies have shown ocean pH marching in step with glacial-interglacial changes in atmospheric CO_2 levels (Hönisch *et al.* 2009), as well as major ocean acidification "events", such as that at the Paleocene-Eocene Thermal Maximum 55 million years ago, that were equal to or greater in magnitude than that observed in the modern instrumental record (Zachos *et al.* 2005). Earth system modeling has played a key role in understanding and constraining these events and understanding the implications for the global carbon cycle (Ridgwell and Schmidt 2010; Ridgwell and Zeebe 2005).

A synthesis of research on known paleo-ocean acidification events (Hönisch *et al.* 2012) concluded that the rate of carbon cycle perturbation has no analog in the past 300 million years of Earth history. While differences exist between the modern and paleo conditions (Doney *et al.* 2009), study of past events can nonetheless provide unique perspective on the long term environmental consequences of, and subsequent recovery from, past ocean acidification events of similar magnitude, if not rate, to what is currently observed (Pelejero *et al.* 2010). It should also be noted that the instrumental record of ocean acidification covers only a few decades, just a fraction of the century-scale anthropogenic CO_2 rise, so paleo proxy-based reconstructions of pH are the only means of establishing a natural, unperturbed baseline. Thus paleo studies may also serve as complement to the ongoing short-term laboratory and field experiments and can extend monitoring records retrospectively.

Paleo-ecological and geochemical research priorities moving forward should include: developing and refining proxies of ocean pH (e.g. boron-based pH estimates) and carbonate saturation state; determining the timescale at which carbon is removed from the system by natural sequestration; predicting how the rates of carbon sediment dissolution may change in response to water column chemical changes and how this will affect water carbonate chemistry; defining the background state of carbonate chemistry (baseline) in the modern and ancient oceans; and determining how organisms and ecosystems responded to and recovered from past ocean acidification events. These research efforts should continue to inform ocean acidification models and vice versa (Theme 3). These geochemical techniques are still largely in development phase and careful calibration and validation studies should commence first, prior to large-scale adoption into a monitoring network.

Laboratories and Field Sites

Shared-use ocean acidification facilities and coordinated field activities are needed for conducting appropriately controlled, manipulative experiments on individual marine species and ecological communities (NRC 2010a). An evaluation of which regions are in need of such facilities and where they might be optimally located should be conducted. Considerations should be given to institutions with a "critical mass" of ocean acidification researchers and intellectual capacity. The development of: "ocean acidification facilities for high-quality carbonate chemistry measurement; FOCE sites; mesocosm facilities; wet labs with well-controlled carbonate chemistry systems; facilities at natural analogue sites; and inter-comparison studies to enable integration of data from different investigators" is critical to ensure the success of future ocean acidification research (NRC 2010). It is also recognized that experimental facilities will have important chemical analytical needs, the technology for which should be co-located at the experimental facilities, especially for sample types that cannot be preserved. Such facilities are needed to allow researchers to mimic natural patterns of variation in the environment, test species responses to ocean acidification, and to allow statistically defensible replication of experiments. Some Federal and academic experimental facilities have been established or are currently being developed (Box 2), but other locations will be required. An inventory of existing and planned Federal and non-federal ocean acidification facilities is strongly advised as a valuable resource for scientists studying the impact of ocean acidification.

Box 2. Examples of Federal and academic experimental and laboratory facilities suitable for ocean acidification research.

Facility	Location
Bodega Marine Laboratory	University of California, Davis, CA
EPA National Health and Enviornmental Effects Research Laboratory	Gulf Breeze, FL, Narragansett, RI, and Newport, OR
EPA Great Lakes National Program Office	Chicago, IL
Friday Harbor Laboratories	University of Washington; Friday Harbor, WA
Hopkins Marine Laboratory	Stanford University; Monterey, CA
Monterey Bay Aquarium Research Institute	Monterey, CA
Mote Marine Laboratory	Sarasota, Florida
NOAA Alaska Fisheries Science Center	Kodiak, AK and Newport, OR
NOAA Northeast Fisheries Science Center	Highlands, NJ and Milford, CT
NOAA Northwest Fisheries Science Center	Seattle, WA
Ocean Acidification Research Center	University of Alaska; Fairbanks, AK

In addition to laboratory and mesocosm facilities, technology to perform ocean experiments in situ should be further planned and implemented. Development of the technology to perform experiments with CO_2 in the ocean is underway at the Monterey Bay Aquarium Research Institute, as part of the FOCE system, but other researchers and institutions are pursuing similar efforts at a smaller scale. Field-based process studies on the impacts of ocean acidification on coral reefs are also currently being conducted by several researchers and institutions in both the Pacific and Atlantic Oceans.

To understand how ocean acidification is and will be affecting U.S. coastal resources, it is recommended that Federal monitoring activities focus on field sites of high resource value. These would be chosen to be part of a suite of ocean acidification intensively studied marine areas which are known to be in vulnerable geographic areas. Existing protected areas, monitoring sites, and laboratories co-located with field sites, should be included in this effort as appropriate (refer to Boxes 2-4 for examples). A list of potential long-term field sites should be generated for the highly characterized geographic regions along the U.S. coasts and a subset selected for targeted ocean acidification monitoring and experimental work. Representative sites should also be identified for each major large marine ecosystem with initial foci on coral reefs and higher latitude systems (e.g., Alaska and the Pacific Northwest). Sites should be in close proximity to observing systems with capacity to characterize the carbonate chemistry of the system. Within these field sites, organisms likely to represent "ecosystem health" should be chosen for monitoring for long-term changes in health and abundance. Developing this list will require additional research on individual species and will not be restricted to calcifying species. These sites may be appropriate for on-site CO_2 manipulative experiments, similar to FOCE and Submersible Habitat for Analyzing Reef Quality (SHARQ, Yates and Halley 2003; See Theme 4, Box 7) experiments conducted in coral reef ecosystems.

Support for Data Synthesis

As the body of observations and data analysis tools derived from the ocean acidification monitoring, research, and modeling activities grows, it will be desirable to conduct periodic synthesis activities. The goal of such syntheses will be to generate readily intelligible information products, such as electronic ocean atlases, that capture the current state of understanding of acidification and its impacts on biogeochemical cycles, organisms, ecosystems, and human activities. A benefit of these analyses will be the identification of weaknesses and gaps that become apparent only after detailed information on the variability of fields has been observed.

Box 3. Examples of initiatives already in place that provide opportunities for long-term ocean acidification research.

The U.S. has a national system of marine protected areas (MPAs) that includes MPA sites, networks, and systems established and managed by Federal, State, territorial, and/or local governments that collectively enhance conservation of the nation's natural and cultural marine heritage, and represent its diverse ecosystems and resources. The national system sites work together at the regional and national levels to achieve common conservation objectives. The national system is administered through the National MPA Center within NOAA; however, each national system MPA continues to be independently managed by its respective entity or entities.

With their place-based focus, long-term data sets, and controlled activities, MPAs are ideal control areas or "sentinel sites" for examining climate change and other impacts including ocean acidification. Real-time results from monitoring programs; advice and feedback from stakeholders; and long-term synthesized information from condition reports all feed into decision-making for an MPA.

In addition to those initiatives, NSF has a program to fund Long-Term Ecological Research (LTER), established in 1980. There are 26 LTER sites representing diverse ecosystems and research emphases and involving more than 1,800 researchers. This program provides ideal opportunities for investigation of long-term impacts of ocean acidification on important marine ecosystems. Moreover, time-series observation sites, such as the Hawaii Ocean Time-series and the Bermuda Atlantic Time-series study sites, have been documenting the process of ocean acidification for more than 20 years through NSF and NOAA funding.

The NOAA Ocean Acidification test-beds which serve as a nexus of in situ research activities that have focused on the impacts of ocean acidification to Atlantic coral reef ecosystems since 2008. A core component of these test-beds is using autonomous measurements of carbon system parameters (see Theme 2) to inform process-based field studies of coral reef ecosystem response (e.g., net calcification, photosynthesis, respiration, benthic community structure) to temporal changes (diurnal, seasonal, annual) in ambient carbonate chemistry. The project unites an interdisciplinary team of investigators from NOAA, USGS, University of Miami, Columbia University, and Woods Hole Oceanographic Institution.

Goals

Research efforts coordinated by the National Ocean Acidification Program should build upon existing research programs and intellectual capacity, as well as ongoing biological and chemical monitoring efforts, to determine physiological responses of marine organisms, examine impacts on marine food webs, and develop indices that track marine ecosystem responses. Research efforts will ultimately enable more comprehensive modeling efforts and facilitate development of appropriate mitigation and adaptation measures. Although specific short- and long-term research priorities are delineated below, it is difficult to assign these topics to timelines as many of the long-term research goals will require work in the short term as well. Most of the research goals listed below are already receiving some attention. The short-term goals represent recommended priorities if funding becomes available. The long-term goals also represent recommended priorities, but they may take longer to yield their full benefits and/or require completion of one or more short-term goals.

Short-term (3-5 years)

- Identify gaps in laboratory and field-site facilities including sites with cultural importance necessary to conduct ocean acidification experiments, and develop appropriate new facilities including FOCE facilities.
- Conduct research to identify potential field sites and candidate species for long-term ecosystem-level monitoring, and subsequently develop and increase their capacity for long-term, ecosystem-level monitoring (in conjunction with efforts described in Theme 2).
- Quantify changes in physiological, developmental, and genetic processes in marine calcifying organisms, including all relevant life history stages, caused by ocean acidification and its interaction with other stressors, giving priority to:
     o Key commercial and culturally important species;
     o Key components of oceanic food chains;
     o Key ecologically important species (e.g., reef-building organisms);
     o Under-studied groups with special need for attention (e.g., cold-water corals); and
     o Organisms using different forms of calcium carbonate structural material in order to understand how responses vary depending on material used.
- Quantify changes in physiological, developmental, and genetic processes on a diversity of marine non-calcifying organisms, including all relevant life history stages and culturally important species, caused by ocean acidification and its interaction with other stressors, with emphasis on establishing baseline data for key species, including:
     o Bacteria and fungi;
     o Primary producers (e.g., macroalgae, phytoplankton, and seagrasses);
     o Invertebrates (e.g., squid, tunicates, and jellies); and
     o Fish and other vertebrates.
- Scale up individual species response research findings to population and ecosystem level response through syntheses and models.
- For all species and ecosystems studies, biologists need to work closely with observing experts (Theme 2) to characterize current natural carbon chemistry (and other characteristics) of source waters so that experimental conditions represent realistic current and future conditions.
- Incorporate findings on individual species' responses into stock assessment and other fishery resource models, as appropriate.
- Develop a candidate list of organisms that can serve as marine ecosystem "sentinels" (using models to inform this choice) for early warning purposes and develop standard operating procedures (SOPs) for their long-term monitoring (in conjunction with efforts described in Theme 2). Biogeochemical parameters may also act as indicators, (e.g., Net Ecosystem Calcification and Net Ecosystem Productivity and DIC:TA ratios in coral reefs, Suzuki and Kawahata 2003; Andersson et al. 2013; Annual Reviews).
- Conduct experiments that address adaptation.
- Quantify changes in key biogeochemical processes at the organism, community, and ecosystem scale that control the cycling of carbon, nitrogen, phosphorus, and sulfur.
- Conduct research on the controlling factors of calcium carbonate dissolution and breakdown including metabolic dissolution and bioerosion.
- Encourage modelers and data collectors to work together, in an iterative fashion, to determine appropriate modeling efforts, and coordinate with data collection efforts.

- Encourage studies focusing on more-vulnerable ecosystems (e.g., coral reefs, high-latitude oceanic environments including Arctic and Antarctic species and ecosystems, and coastal environments), including those affected by multiple anthropogenic and environmental stressors.
- Encourage and facilitate international research activities and scientific exchanges (in conjunction with efforts described in Theme 6).
- Evaluate biogeochemical proxies of ocean acidification and organism response, with emphasis on calibration and multiple-proxy techniques.
- Collect and evaluate historical records (e.g., core-based studies) of organism and ecosystem response to historical changes in ocean chemistry using a combination of paleo-ecological and geochemical proxy techniques.
- Continue ongoing investigations of the effects of CO_2- and pH-driven changes on the transfer of carbon from the ocean surface to its depths (i.e., the biological pump).
- Continue ongoing investigations to determine how ocean acidification may alter the nitrogen, iron, phosphorous, silicate, oxygen, and sulfur cycles and their interactions with marine ecosystems.
- Conduct research on the solubility and rate (kinetics) of dissolution of metastable calcium carbonate minerals, sediments and structures, and how rates may change in response to water column chemical changes and how this will affect water carbonate chemistry.
- Conduct regular (approximately every 3 years) data synthesis to take stock of findings and set new priorities.

Long-term (10 years)
- Continue progress from the short-term goals.
- Ensure that research addresses knowledge gaps related to more vulnerable systems (e.g., coral reefs, high-latitude oceanic environments, and coastal environments, including estuaries).
- Build an understanding of why organisms respond differently to ocean acidification with respect to:
    - oPhysiology and response mechanisms;
    - oMineralogy of calcifying species; and
    - oGene expression.
- Investigate the potential for physiological acclimation and epigenetic effects and examine evolutionary mechanisms for adaptation to maintain or increase ecosystem resilience, with emphasis on culturally, ecologically, and economically important organisms.
- Investigate how changes at the organism level will alter ecosystem structure and function using techniques that include evolutionary genetics, laboratory, field, and mesocosm experiments on single and multi-species assemblages.
- Investigate cumulative or synergistic effects of ocean acidification with other stressors, including increased ocean temperatures and eutrophication.

Budget
The FY 2012 Budget allocated $12.76 million to support research efforts under the National Ocean Acidification Program, as described in Theme 1 (see Appendix 2 for more details). Agencies presently supporting ocean acidification research efforts include NASA, NOAA, NSF, and USGS.

Theme 2. Monitoring of Ocean Chemistry and Biological Impacts

In order to support the research objectives described in Theme 1 and to document the status and progress of ocean acidification in estuarine, coastal, and open-ocean environments, and to understand its drivers and impacts on marine ecosystems, it will be necessary to develop a coordinated multidisciplinary multinational approach for observations and modeling that will be fundamental to establishing a successful research strategy for ocean acidification. This will facilitate the development of our capability to predict present-day and future responses of marine biota, ecosystem processes, biogeochemistry, and climate change feedbacks. Required research elements include regional and global networks of observations collected in concert with process studies, manipulative experiments, field studies, and modeling. Local and regional observation networks will provide the necessary data required to firmly establish impacts attributable to ocean acidification. Monitoring of the oceans on appropriate temporal and spatial scales is critical to understanding ocean acidification and associated environmental changes. Carbonate chemistry observations are required to address ocean acidification in open-ocean locations through the global oceanic carbon observatory network of repeat hydrographic surveys, time-series stations (ship-based and moored), and ship-based underway surface observations in the Atlantic, Pacific, and Indian Oceans. Carbon observing networks do not, however, exist for coastal and estuarine environments. Enhancing open-ocean carbon monitoring activities and expanding these networks into coastal and estuarine regions is essential to understanding and predicting responses of marine biota to ocean acidification, as well as changes in ecosystem processes, biogeochemistry, and climate feedbacks.

Requirements and Recommendations

Determining the changes in seawater chemistry and biology in a rising CO_2 world is vital for understanding the ecosystems changes that will ultimately control the size and composition of our fisheries and other biological resources. Ocean acidification monitoring and research focuses on four carbon parameters: partial pressure of carbon dioxide (pCO_2), pH, TA, and dissolved inorganic carbon (DIC). Monitoring efforts should measure a minimum of two of these parameters to allow determination of all carbon species and to ensure internal consistency of the data. These parameters, as well as temperature, salinity, oxygen, nutrients, dissolved organic carbon (DOC), and particulate organic and inorganic carbon (POC, PIC), can be measured routinely onboard ships. Data for these same parameters should be collected from open-ocean, coastal, and estuarine waters. While some portion of these chemical species now can be measured on moorings and floats in open water systems, they are not yet broadly utilized on a global scale including coastal and estuarine systems. The chemical measurements described above are critical for validation of sensors, development of proxy methods, and assessment of accuracies.

To assess the biological response to ocean acidification in oceans and coasts, the following biological measurements should be made as part of the monitoring effort:
* Biomass of functional groups:
    o Phytoplankton (including timing of bloom, community shifts, and pigments)
    o Zooplankton, both micro- (e.g., protists) and meso- (i.e., multicellular and including meroplankton)
    o Microbes
    o Benthic animals, algae, and plants in coastal regions

These measurements need to be made with the contemporaneous physical and chemical measurements for ocean acidification defined above. Methods for biota biomass measurements may include acoustics, pigment analysis, and flow cytometry. Biomass of calcified versus non-calcified species is desired.

Primary production, carbon and nitrogen fixation, metabolism, respiration, and biological species composition are also important biological measurements to correlate with chemical indicators of ocean acidification.

Some of these processes may interact in seawater to enhance or reduce acidification in many coastal environments (Feely *et al.* 2012). Correlations may provide insight to population- and community-level effects and could ultimately lead to development of biological indicators. The National Ocean Acidification Program will need to incorporate a process for identifying issues to be addressed by biological indicators (Theme 1) and guidelines for developing the indicators and vetting their performance (e.g., Jackson *et al.* 2000; Theme 4). Of particular importance is development of indicators that characterize biological effects with major long-term ecological or economic consequences, are responsive to ocean acidification over other environmental variables, have the power to detect meaningful differences, and can be applied at fairly broad spatial scales with relatively low cost. As biological indicators are developed and integrated with process studies (Theme 1), they will need to be adapted into long-term field monitoring plans (NRC 2010a; Feely *et al.* 2012). For example, in coral reef ecosystems, biogeochemical parameters such as the relative magnitude of net ecosystem organic carbon production and net ecosystem calcification, which can be deducted from chemical measurements of DIC and TA, may serve as potential indicators of ecosystem performance and health (Suzuki and Kawahata 2003; Andersson and Gledhill 2013).

Strategy for Coordinating an Observational Network for Ocean Acidification

Many of the same sampling principles and strategies that are being developed for open-ocean and coastal carbon and biogeochemical repeat hydrographic surveys and time-series stations apply to the development of an observational network for ocean acidification. Consequently, most of the planning towards integrating hydrographic surveys and time-series measurements should be focused into a single coordinated effort using the interagency resources and infrastructures that presently exist for high-latitude regions, warm and cold water coral reefs, coastal regions including estuaries, and tropical/subtropical pelagic regions. Monitoring in these regions reflects the need to better understand global variations in ocean sensitivity to acidification. Regions with strong upwelling regimes (such as the U.S. West Coast) could be more vulnerable, because upwelled waters are naturally higher in CO_2 (and thus lower in pH); coastal regions with high freshwater input from rivers may also be more vulnerable to acidification because fresh water has a decreased ability to neutralize acids, in general, and may carry other acidifying solutes. In urbanized coastal regions, local sources of chemical species other than CO_2 (e.g., nitrogen and sulfur oxides, organic matter, nutrients, etc) can also contribute to the local acidification processes (Cai *et al.* 2011; Feely *et al.* 2012; Sunda and Cai 2012; Feely *et al.* 2012). Ocean acidification may be exacerbated in polar ecosystems, as CO_2 is more soluble in colder water, and the loss of sea ice in summer results in greater exposure of seawater to the atmosphere, potentially allowing for more, but variable (Semiletov *et al.* 2007), exchange of CO_2 across the ocean-atmosphere interface. Fresh water dilution, from arctic ice melt, at high latitudes also exacerbates acidification and results in under-saturation of carbonate minerals. However, it should be noted that low-latitude systems are not immune to such changes. In fact, the greatest rate of change in seawater carbonate mineral saturation state has been observed within the Atlantic tropical waters where coral growth rates and declines in proportion to changing carbonate mineral saturation state are already being observed (NOAA 2010a). Additionally, the U.S. efforts should coordinate and collaborate with international activities as appropriate (Theme 6).

Additional chemical and biological measurements, such as highly resolved depth distributions and abundances of calcifying plankton, estimates of $CaCO_3$ calcification and dissolution rates, and other CO_2-sensitive processes as appropriate, should be added to existing repeat surveys to monitor ocean acidification and its associated impacts. Likewise, opportunities for development of new long-term monitoring systems should be explored to fill any data collection gaps identified in priority areas such as high-latitude regions, warm and cold water coral reefs, and coastal regions and estuaries. Plans are underway for developing coordinated monitoring networks at the regional, national and international levels (Newton *et al.* in preparation). These coordinated observing systems will build on presently existing carbon and biogeochemistry monitoring networks and add appropriate chemical and biological sensors to address acidification issues. The monitoring efforts will be conducted by individual nations coordinated through the auspices of the International Ocean Carbon Coordination Project.

The sampling plans for the next phase of the World Climate Research Programme's (WCRP) CLIVAR CO_2 Repeat Hydrography Program (also referred to as Global Ocean Ship-based Hydrographic Investigations

Program) can effectively provide the required long timescale information for the ocean acidification network (Figure 4). Spatial sampling should continue to repeat the transect lines carried out in the Atlantic, Pacific, and Indian Oceans, with the Southern Ocean integrated as part of the other basins. The Arctic is of increasing importance and should be emphasized (Robbins *et al.* 2010) by establishing a monitoring effort in appropriate locales.

The Chukchi and Beaufort Seas in the western Arctic Ocean are undergoing a rapid transition as sea ice duration and extent diminish as atmospheric and oceanic temperatures continue to increase. The changes in sea ice cover are having a profound effect on the carbonate chemistry in the region. The removal of perennial sea ice from the Canada Basin has allowed an unprecedented uptake of CO_2 from the atmosphere since 2007, causing a rapid equilibration between the surface ocean and the atmosphere. Additionally, the presence of ice melt water, which has low concentrations of carbonate species, has caused aragonite to become undersaturated during summer and fall months across wide areas (Mathis *et al.* 2012). Over the highly productive Chukchi shelf, the uncoupling between primary production and grazing rates of zooplankton leads to high export of organic carbon from the surface to the bottom where it is remineralized, increasing the local acidity (Mathis *et al.*, submitted).

For shallow water coastal and estuarine environments and areas inaccessible by open-ocean ships, a similar sampling strategy, as outlined for the open-ocean carbon measurements, is recommended, but at much higher temporal and spatial resolution than for the open ocean. These activities will be integrated with ongoing ship-based surveys in coastal areas, but at higher frequencies as required (hourly for time-series measurements). Federal agencies should encourage state and regional entities, including the tribal nations, to add ocean acidification monitoring to the existing coastal and estuarine water quality monitoring programs. This monitoring may also lead to development of acidification source budgets for these waters which are heavily influenced by land-based activities (Feely *et al.* 2012).

Underway sampling on research vessels and Voluntary Observing Ships (VOS) from the U.S. and other countries should be taken advantage of by including the additional pH, carbon, and biological parameters necessary to address ocean acidification and acidification impacts (Figure 5). These data would help establish large-scale trends in ocean acidification in much the same way as established basin-scale trends in pCO_2. Additional biological parameters, including those identified by ongoing and future research (Theme 1), should be included to assess ecosystem responses to ocean acidification (see above).

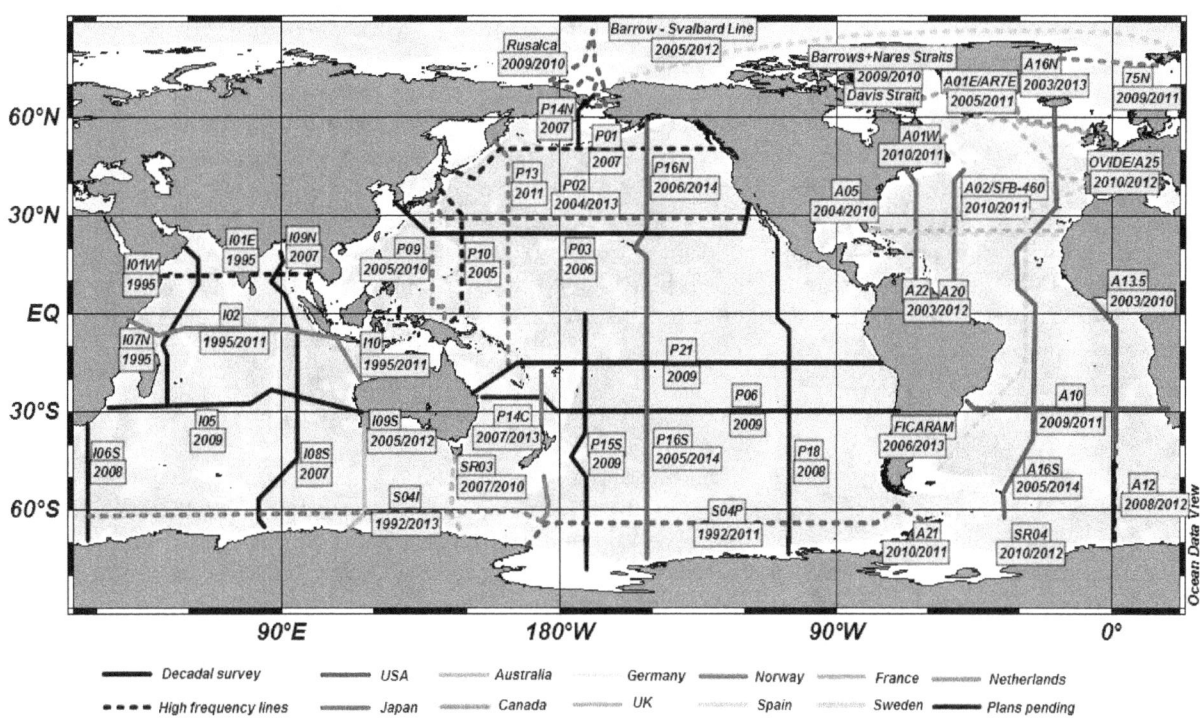

Figure 4. Planned Climate Variability and Predictability (CLIVAR) CO_2 Repeat Hydrography surveys and high-frequency lines for carbon and ocean acidification measurements

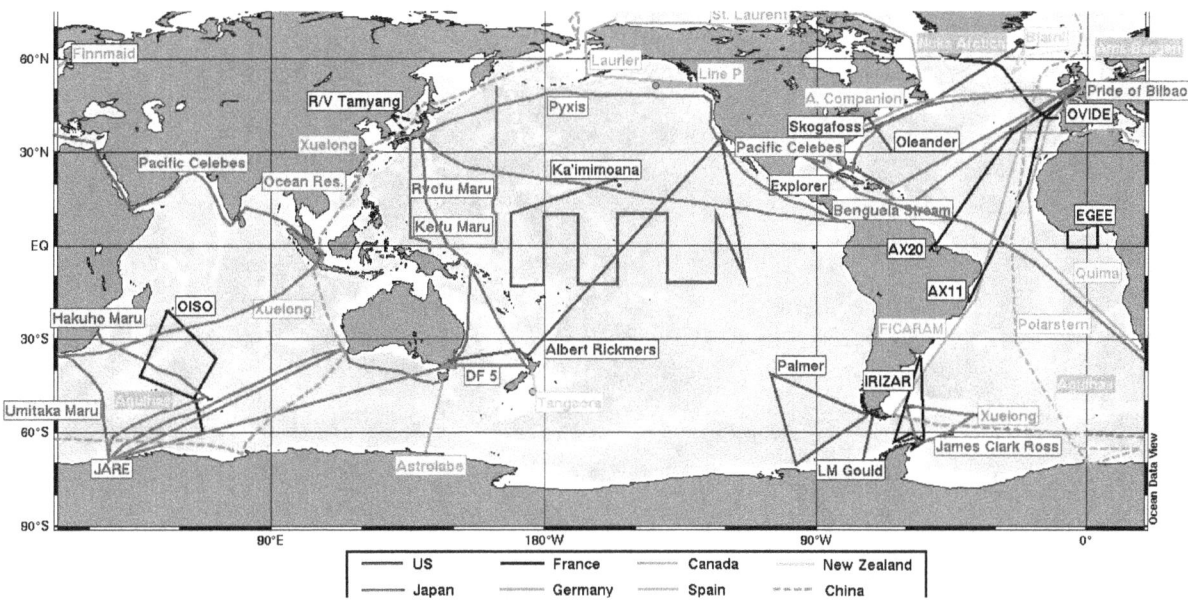

Figure 5. Planned underway voluntary observing ship (VOS) surveys for surface ocean measurements of pCO_2 and other carbon and biological parameters

Time-series Measurements at Fixed Stations

Time-series stations are urgently needed in the open-ocean, coastal regions, and estuaries to document high frequency (hourly) variations in ocean acidification relevant parameters (Figure 6; e.g., Dore *et al.* 2009). Existing observing systems that are already conducting time-series measurements should be given priority for inclusion in the ocean acidification monitoring program if their location is also justified scientifically (refer to Box 4 for examples). By enhancing a subset of these time-series locations with the appropriate chemical and biological sensors, an ocean acidification network can be developed at reasonable costs. Nonetheless, the main criteria should be guided by the scientific rationale, which will require deployment of new observing systems, for example, in the coastal ocean where less is understood about the temporal and spatial variability of acidification. Buoys in existing programs should be equipped with carbon system sensors for ocean acidification. Additionally, bio-optical sensors and optical plankton imaging systems should be deployed to track possible shifts in abundances of key biological functional groups (e.g., calcifying phytoplankton and pteropods). Seasonal measurements of calcification rates and other CO_2-sensitive processes not currently measured at time-series sites are necessary to assess the long-term response of ecosystems to ocean acidification.

In addition to expanding ocean acidification monitoring into existing monitoring networks, efforts should be placed on the compilation and interpretation of the existing historic datasets. The OCB4 recommended that the EPA "seek out long-term coastal States' and Federal datasets (e.g., USGS, NOAA) on water quality or any monitoring studies that have included pH data collected in coastal State waters." These data may provide information on the natural variability within estuarine and coastal systems and the dominant factors influencing pH in different types of estuaries. This long-term data could appropriately inform planned acidification monitoring sites. For example, the EPA and other agencies have been collecting pH data throughout the Great Lakes at sites at or in close proximity to purposed monitoring locations for several decades (NOAA, 2010a).

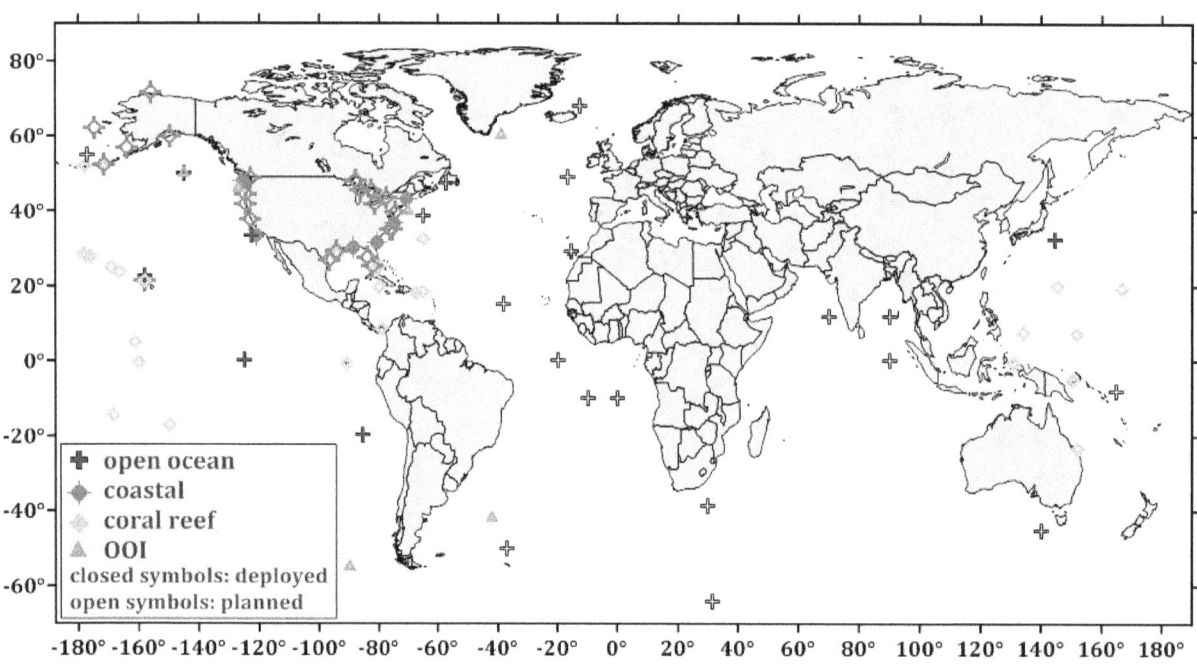

Figure 6. Planned U.S. carbon and acidification monitoring sites in open-ocean, coastal ocean, and coral reef regions for time-series measurements and process studies (from NOAA Ocean and Great Lakes Acidification Research Plan, April 2010; refer to Feely et al. 2010 for information on internationally coordinated moorings).

Box 4. Examples of existing, major observing programs that collect time-series measurements at fixed stations and could be augmented with ocean acidification measurements.

- OceanSITES is a worldwide system of long-term, deepwater reference stations that measure dozens of variables and monitor the full depth of the ocean with 30 surface and 30 subsurface arrays. OceanSITES moorings are an integral part of the Global Ocean Observing System. Satellite telemetry enables near real-time access to OceanSITES data by scientists and the public.

- The Ocean Observatories Initiative (OOI) is constructing a networked infrastructure of science-driven sensor systems to measure physical, chemical, geological, and biological variables in the ocean and seafloor. The network will include coastal and open-ocean assets adjacent to the U.S., as well as global assets elsewhere in the world's oceans, particularly the high latitudes.

- The Integrated Ocean Observing System (IOOS) is a Federal, regional, and private-sector partnership that collects and delivers valuable oceanographic data along our coasts.

- The National Association of Marine Laboratories (NAML) is a nonprofit organization representing marine and Great Lakes laboratories. Member institutions have long-term data sets for various physical and biological parameters as measured from docks, water intake systems, or frequently monitored shallow-water sites.

- The EPA National Estuary Program (NEP) is a Federal program established to improve the quality of 28 estuaries of national importance distributed across the U.S. coastline. The EPA works with States to maintain high water quality in these estuaries and can incorporate new instrumentation and methods for monitoring acidification and its effects in estuaries.

- The NOAA/National Ocean Service (NOS) National Estuarine Research Reserve System (NERRS) is a network of protected areas in U.S. coastal regions with long-term water quality monitoring systems designed to monitor physical, chemical, and biological parameters.

- The NOAA/National Ocean Service (NOS) National Marine Sanctuary Program (NMSP) is comprised of 14 marine protected areas. NMSP monitoring activities are comprised of efforts targeting individual and multiple sites, including the System-Wide Monitoring Program (SWiM).

- The Long-Term Ecological Research (LTER) Network is supported by the National Science Foundation and is used to study ecological processes over long temporal and broad spatial scales at a variety of land-based and marine locations. Some of the marine sites are suitable for monitoring ocean acidification processes.

- The NOAA Coral Reef Conservation Program (CRCP) maintains a set of time-series stations and satellite observations to provide coral reef managers, scientists, and other users worldwide with information and forecasts of coral bleaching events using sea surface temperature data. The CRCP now in partnership with NOAA's Ocean Acidification Program includes ocean acidification as a key element comprising both geochemical and ecological metrics specific to tracking the status and trend of ocean acidification within U.S. coral reef environments.

- The National Park Service Inventory and Monitoring (I&M) Program provides a set of 12 baseline natural resource inventories in National Parks, which include coastal and estuarine locations. Natural resource inventories are extensive point-in-time surveys to determine the location or condition of a resource, including the presence, class, distribution, and status of biological resources such as plants and animals and abiotic resources such as air, water, soils, and climate in certain coastal and estuarine locations. The NPS I&M Vital Signs Monitoring Program measures physical and biological indicators of ecosystem condition across networks of parks in bioregions.

Box 4. Continued

- The FWS National Wildlife Refuge System Inventory and Monitoring (I&M) Initiative will includes a suite of monitoring parameters to assess impacts of increasing seawater pH on coral organisms and other reef-building species located on National Wildlife Refuges throughout the U.S., particularly in the remote Pacific Ocean. The I&M Initiative will also monitor the health and reproductive success of nesting seabirds which could prove to be a useful surrogate for assessing changes in the open ocean food web. Many of these refuges are located far from most human-caused stressors and are free from disturbance from commercial fishing making them ideal natural laboratories for monitoring the effects ocean acidification.

- The EPA Great Lakes Monitoring program conducts a bi-annual survey of the water column in approximately 20 locations in each of the Great Lakes. pH and alkalinity are measured, but the glass electrode-based pH methodology used has low precision and would need to be improved for monitoring of long-term trends due to carbon acidification. This program could be further augmented by collecting water samples for laboratory-based DIC and alkalinity measurements.

Time-series Measurements on Floats and Gliders

Developing new technologies to enhance chemical and biological sensors on floats and gliders should be supported (Theme 4). Carbon and pH sensors on autonomous floats and gliders could resolve shorter space-time scale variability of the upper ocean more readily than repeat sections and could provide access to shallower waters than most ships, but the sensor technology must be developed and tested in the field before it can be implemented on a large scale (Theme 4). In the meantime, the addition of oxygen sensors would rapidly and inexpensively enhance the biogeochemical relevance of existing floats (such as those in the Argo Program). The data could be utilized to directly address ocean acidification issues via appropriate algorithm development (Juranek *et al.* 2009, 2011; Alin *et al.* 2012). Further development of these sensor packages and algorithms for ocean acidification will be emphasized and coordinated with satellite remote sensing activities (below).

Remote Sensing

Satellites can provide synoptic observations of a range of physical and optical parameters that allow us to model changes in the distribution of carbonate chemistry within the surface ocean where no in situ observations are available. Through the application of a variety of techniques, satellite observations are being applied to extend in situ carbonate chemistry measurements over broader scales, permitting examination on spatial and temporal scales not practical through in situ observations alone (e.g., Gledhill *et al.* 2008). The success of local algorithms to predict episodic events (Juranek *et al.* 2009; Alin *et al.* 2012) could potentially be extended using satellite remote sensing. Remote sensing has also had success observing important classes of phytoplankton (e.g., calcifying species known as coccolithophorids) that strongly interact with the carbonate cycle and will be directly affected by ocean acidification (Balch *et al.* 2007).

Goals

The National Ocean Acidification Program monitoring plan should be designed to rapidly characterize the magnitude and extent of acidification through a comprehensive monitoring effort at global, regional, and local scales. This information is required to develop robust ecological, economic, and cultural projections of future impacts of ocean acidification in order for policy makers, managers, and local stakeholders to make informed decisions (NRC 2010a; Ocean Research and Resources Advisory Panel [ORRAP] 2010). The monitoring plan should be designed to maximize collaborations and thus leverage planned and existing observing assets, nationally and internationally. Most of the monitoring goals listed below are receiving some attention already.

The short-term goals represent recommended priorities if funding becomes available. The long-term goals also represent recommended priorities, but they may take longer to yield their full benefits and/or require completion of one or more short-term goals.

Short-term (3-5 years)

*   Evaluate the geographical extent and capabilities of existing monitoring systems in regions and habitats where ocean acidification effects are most likely to occur and subsequently identify:
    *   oSystems which should be utilized and expanded; and
    *   oRegions and habitats where new systems may be warranted.
*   Expand existing coastal and ocean measurements by deploying new ocean acidification monitoring instrumentation on research ships, volunteer observing ships, moorings, floats, and gliders.
*   Identify and deploy monitoring instrumentation in coastal and estuarine sites to extend the open-ocean monitoring parameters and methods to these shallow water systems. Work closely with regional and state entities to develop monitoring programs for ocean acidification in state/tribal waters. Assist these entities in developing source budgets to quantify relative contributions of atmospheric versus land-based sources of acidification.
*   Document trends in ocean acidification physical, chemical, and biological responses that can be used for real-time early warning systems and for verification of computer model outputs.
*   Improve adoption of standardized chemical, physical, and biological monitoring protocols.
*   Develop new technology that will allow for accurate in situ measurements of the carbon system and biological responses (Theme 4).
*   Synthesize observing data in an effort to describe and explain acidification status of U.S. waters, likely with a regional focus.
*   Integrate observational data into regional and global models.
*   Foster closer connections between observing scientists and biologists in order to provide pertinent information about carbon chemistry of waters where species being studied reside naturally.
*   Develop biological monitoring protocols.

Long-term (10 years)

*   Expand and complete ocean acidification global monitoring network.
*   Expand and complete ocean acidification network for coastal regions and estuaries.
*   Continue development of biological monitoring protocols.
*   Integrate new protocols into global monitoring system.
*   Integrate models of biogeochemical processes with ecosystem forecasts.

Budget

The FY 2012 Budget allocated $6.3 million to support the monitoring efforts for the National Ocean Acidification Program, as described above in Theme 2 (see Appendix 2 for more details). Agencies presently supporting ocean acidification monitoring efforts include NASA, NOAA, NSF, and USGS. New chemical and biological ocean acidification sensors would be deployed on research cruises, moorings, gliders, and floats. The overall number of deployed sensors would increase over time and be maintained for the duration of the program.

Theme 3. Modeling to Predict Changes in the Ocean Carbon Cycle and Impacts on Marine Ecosystems and Organisms

Ocean modeling has progressed rapidly during recent decades with the inclusion of biogeochemical models embedded in three-dimensional general circulation models. The biogeochemistry ocean general circulation model (BOGCM) community has progressed towards simulations of the global carbon cycle, and ultimately towards a predictive capacity that includes changes in the carbon cycle as a function of changes in global temperature, ocean circulation, ocean biogeochemistry, and terrestrial and atmospheric inputs. For instance, Steinacher *et al.* (2009) realistically represented DIC and saturation state aragonite (Ωarag), a mineral phase of calcium carbonate, for the surface global ocean, and then projected those parameters forward for the Arctic in 2100 (Box 5). The BOGCM community has made strong progress towards incorporating aspects of the carbonate cycle into modeling frameworks and continues to improve its ability to realistically capture experimental results within models.

In contrast, the incorporation of realistic biological ocean properties, conditions, and parameters into BOGCMs to examine ocean acidification is still in the very early stages, which largely reflects the broader state of the field rather than solely the status for ocean acidification. At this point, scientific understanding of the responses of organisms to ocean acidification is limited (Theme 1), making it difficult to understand and model organismal response to an acidifying ocean. New approaches such as trait-based modeling that permit exploration of the capacity of entire communities of species to adapt to environmental change (e.g., Follows *et al.* 2007) or individual-based models that have explicit descriptions of species behavior, have strong potential for ocean acidification modeling. There are significant scaling issues that complicate linkage of BOGCMs with finer scales of ecological organization and with higher frequency variation and spatial heterogeneity of coastal environments. Solutions to these scaling problems will both inform and depend upon results from observation programs and biological/ecological studies (Theme 1). Ultimately, these issues are not specific to ocean modeling, but to all attempts to identify and capture appropriate scales of ecosystem complexity in a computer model and then project how the system will respond (e.g., Gilman *et al.* 2010).

There is a need for models that can provide for ocean resource management and decision support by addressing acclimation and adaptation issues, including habitat shifts and invasions at both global and regional levels. Regional models are especially needed for high-latitude open-oceans, coral reefs, and coastal regions, which are all vulnerable to ocean acidification in the near-term. Considerable progress is required to reach this level of accuracy because decision support often requires shorter time- and spatial-scales (i.e., shorter data latency) than many current three-dimensional models can realistically provide. Some types of decision support can best be provided by empirical models (e.g., regression) rather than by utilizing Regional Ocean Modeling Systems (ROMS), which have a more limited spatial domain than BOGCMs but lack the necessary operational capability for management and decision support. Empirical models, however, are ineffective for extrapolations beyond a few days and they lack the capability to provide new insights for ecological interactions or climate alterations. There is a general need for developing adequate regional models, such as ROMS or Finite Volume Community Ocean Models that are nested within, or use output from BOGCMs, in order to manage a variable and changing climate and for human adaptation to climate change. These regional-scale hydrodynamic models are frequently integrated into estuarine water quality models for decision support under the Clean Water Act. Thus, investment in this area of modeling in the near future is a necessity to understand these complex intersecting systems through differing scales of observation (Theme 2) and biotic response research (Theme 1) that are applied to them. Similarly, there is strong interest in Integrated Assessment Models (IAMs) that are primarily econometric (Theme 5), but have increasingly included ecological components to capture the interaction between ecosystems and economics (Box 6). Such models have not yet been applied to ocean acidification impacts on coastal economies. Ultimately, the model being used will depend on the research question being asked.

Box 5. Global carbonate modeling

Aragonite is a form of calcium carbonate ($CaCO_3$) used by organisms such as calcifying algae, bivalves, corals, and foraminifera to produce shells and other structures. Under the IPCC emission scenario A2 (Metz *et al.* 2007), global surface waters currently suitable for calcification by aragonitic organisms will disappear in the Arctic by 2070, coinciding with a pH decrease of 0.45 (Steinacher *et al.* 2009), which would lead to widespread aragonite undersaturation (i.e., Ωarag values less than 1). Under the scenario in which the world chooses consistently and effectively a development path that favors efficiency of resource use and "dematerialization" of economic activities (IPCC scenario B1), the mean Ωarag of surface waters will still likely decrease from 3.4 (pre-industrial level) to 2.3 by the end of the century. The authors highlighted several model deficiencies such as the lack of feedback between carbonate state variables and the biological carbon cycle (Steinacher *et al.* 2009). Feeley *et al.* (2009) also modeled global aragonite saturation, and their results predict that only tropical and subtropical waters will be able to support growth of calcifying organisms by the end of the 21st Century. A subset of their results are depicted below:

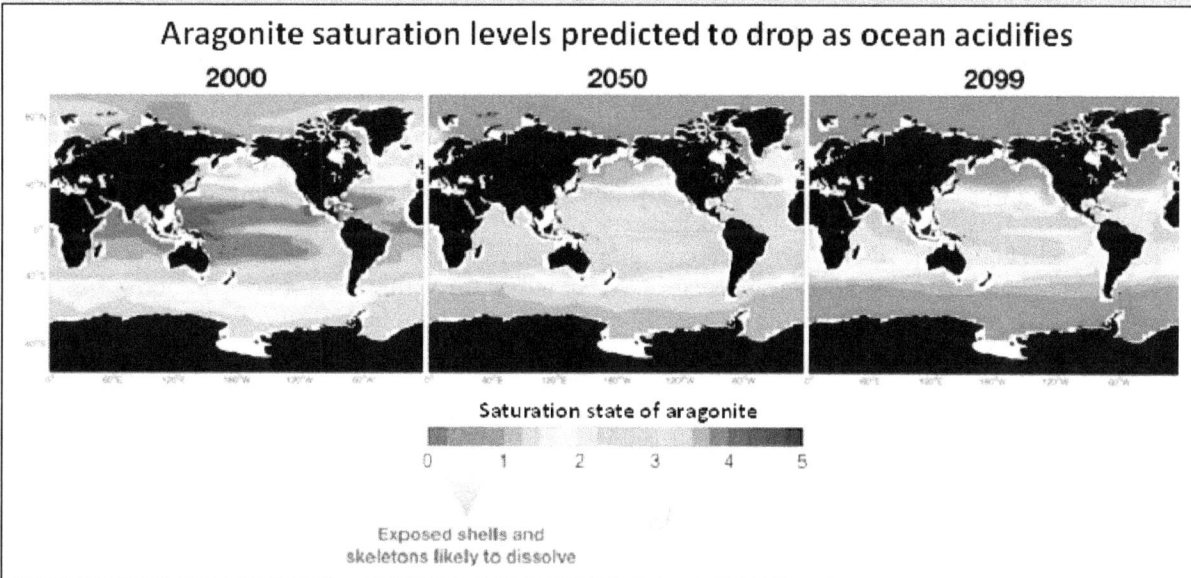

Model-calculated aragonite saturation states throughout the surface ocean in 2000, 2050, and 2099 (From Oceanus, January 2010; adapted for Oceanus from Feely et al. 2009; designed by Katherine Joyce, Woods Hole Oceanographic Institution). Surface values were calculated with the National Center for Atmospheric Research's Community Climate System Model 3.1. Most exposed aragonite structures (corals, shells, etc.) will dissolve in regions where the aragonite saturation state is below 1 (shades of red). Growth of calcifying organisms may decrease with declining saturation state, even if it remains above 1 (Feely et al. 2009).

Box 6. Integrated Assessment Modeling

Integrated assessment models (IAMs) link models of different systems to assess how changes in one of the modeled systems are likely to affect outcomes in one or more of the linked systems. The most prevalent examples of IAMs are those that assess the socioeconomic impacts of climate change. Climate IAMs link one output of economic activity, greenhouse gas emissions, to Earth systems models that represent the atmospheric dynamics that ultimately contribute to climate change. Changes in the Earth's climate will impact things like food production, human health, and sea level rise. An economic model then operates on the outcome of these processes

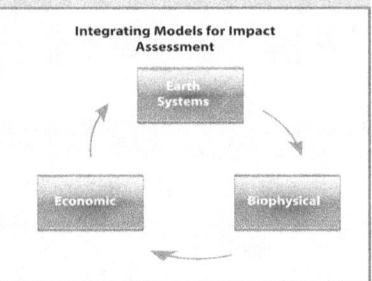

to forecast changes in social welfare and economic productivity which, in turn, influences the emissions of greenhouse gases. Thus the linking of dynamic models from different academic disciplines can provide valuable insight to policy makers. An analogous IAM for the causes and consequences of ocean acidification will require linking models of the atmospheric, terrestrial, and ocean carbon cycles, the biophysical processes by which changes in temperature and ocean chemistry affect the flow of marine ecosystem services, and, finally, an economic model that determines how social welfare and economic productivity are expected to change as a result.

Requirements and Recommendations

Recommendations are based on the NRC Report (2010a), Oschlies et al. (2010), and Fabry et al. (2008). There is a general need for more integration of biogeochemical models with ecosystem/food web models via mechanistic relationships. Progress has already been made in merging these two classes of models with programs such as Integrated Marine Biogeochemistry and Ecosystem Research (IMBER) making it a focus area, but further efforts are needed to understand the utility of the various approaches. Recommendations for modeling with respect to ocean acidification include:

- Develop physiology-based models that describe organismal response to ocean acidification and extend beyond single parameter response (e.g., calcification) to include growth and reproductive success.
- Target specific keystone or economic species. Increased efforts to examine effects of ocean acidification on individual species should focus on keystone, economically and culturally important species, and subsistence species in different ecosystems. Clearly, managing various fisheries species specifically sensitive to an acidifying ocean, including algae, mollusks, crustaceans, and fish, will require an understanding of ocean acidification effects (Theme 1), which will need to be captured in models validated through field observations (Theme 2) to determine potential ecological, cultural, and economic impacts and support resource managers. Develop models of impacts to exceptionally vulnerable species, communities, and geographic areas in order to inform prioritization of research.
- Incorporate more detailed life history strategies of specific organisms at higher trophic levels. In most BOGCMs, zooplankton are the highest trophic level, whereas in fisheries models, they are the lowest after the primary producers, making zooplankton a crucial link. Although knowledge and parameterization of zooplankton and larval fish sensitivity to ocean acidification is limited, and end-to-end food web modeling is still a nascent field, improved ability to capture these aspects is critical for projecting effects of ocean acidification on ocean ecology.
- Develop an understanding of the interactions between ocean acidification, oxygen concentration, atmospheric inputs, and temperature, which are all affected by climate change. This is needed for all of the oceans, but it is compelling for the Pacific and Arctic Oceans, which are already experiencing large increases in temperature and diminished aragonite saturation due to ocean acidification.
- Incorporate improved representations of remineralization processes, especially in the depth zone just beneath the surface, sunlit layer (i.e., the "twilight zone"). This will also require connecting "ballast" export flux and organism biology, because particle size and composition and trophic interactions affect the sinking rate and extent of remineralization in the water column.
- Refine and select appropriate parameterizations for PIC and couple it with carbonate chemistry, rather than treating them independently.
- Use total alkalinity (TA) as a prognostic tracer rather than a diagnostic from salinity. TA is a key

component of the carbonate system, but models often calculate it as a constant function of salinity. It should be directly calculated so that its effect on organisms can be accurately defined.

- Address needs specific to estuaries and coastal regions, including:
  o Develop an increased capacity for regional downscaling to study regional effects of global forcings. Climate forecasts are necessarily done at the global scale, but modeling local environments that contain specific ecology and conditions (e.g., coral reefs, nearshore habitats, the Arctic and Southern Oceans) requires coupling global drivers to the regional grid-scale.

  oUse high-resolution regional models to realistically represent coastal upwelling or coral reef hydrodynamics that are smaller than the grid-scale of global models.

Ocean Acidification may make it difficult for echinoderms like this Bahama sea star to build their skeletons. credit: Courtney Barry

  oCouple current sophisticated terrestrial land-use/land-use-change models with coastal hydrology to provide critical information for regions where most of the populations resides. Currently, coastal models often only include crude representations of river inputs or estuarine circulation, thus limiting our ability to understand the influence of terrestrial forcing from land use changes or to capture important benthic-pelagic coupling in shallow ecosystems.

  oDevelop IAMs and other appropriate food web and ecosystem models to forecast impacts of ocean acidification on coastal fisheries and economies.

  oDevelop models that will differentiate natural and anthropogenic CO_2 sources (i.e., atmospheric CO_2 and respiration-derived CO_2 from human-induced eutrophication).

Overarching recommendations for improving the overall modeling endeavor include:

- Use models to guide observational sampling strategies (Themes 1 and 2). Observing System Simulation Experiments (OSSEs) are widely used in some fields to plan the most effective and efficient design for sampling, but they have scarcely been applied to marine science.
- Provide formal estimation and treatment, especially in decision-applications, of uncertainty arising from measurement error, structural error (i.e., model uncertainty), and any remaining untested assumptions.
- Adequately archive model code (addressed in Theme 7).
- Document model skill assessment (evaluation metrics) in modeling reports. Skill assessments should seek to quantify uncertainty and inform solutions to model scaling challenges through rigorous consideration of trade-offs between model accuracy and model precision.

Goals
The incorporation of realistic biological parameters into global ocean models and development of regional and coastal models are essential to understanding and planning for the effects of ocean acidification on ecosystems and human society. Many of the ocean acidification modeling goals listed below are receiving some investment already. The short-term goals represent recommended priorities if funding becomes available. The long-term goals also represent recommended priorities, but they may take longer to yield their full benefits and/or require completion of one or more short-term goals. Many modeling goals are limited by the availability of experimental results that will arise from the other themes of this strategic plan. With that caveat, and awareness of tremendous amounts of ongoing efforts worldwide to provide the relevant understanding, the goals are:

Short-term (3-5 years)
- Develop and improve models less complex than end-to-end models that can predict direct and indirect effects on culturally, economically, and ecologically important species and processes.
- Strengthen ocean biology life history and trophic couplings in end-to-end models.
- Explore use of OSSEs for in situ and remote/satellite and aircraft-based ocean acidification observation network design.
- Identify and track regional modeling efforts (e.g., water quality models) that include or could be expanded to include carbonate chemistry.
- Continue progress on nesting downscaled regional models within global climate models to ensure an understanding and predictive capability of the impact of a variable and changing climate on ocean biology (adaptation).
- Expand implementation of alkalinity as a tracer and incorporation of PIC and remineralization formulations in BOGCMs.

Long-term (10 years)
- Continue progress from the short-term goals, and revise near-term priorities as needed based on progress.
- Invest in and develop multi- and interdisciplinary models to ensure coupling of coastal processes on both sides of the land-ocean boundary, as well as atmospheric processes.
- As an intermediate step toward the above goal, confront and evaluate downscaled and regional models with new observation data (see short-term goals under Theme 2).
- Ensure adequate Federal capacity for archiving model code and results (in conjunction with efforts described in Theme 7) to support management and decision making; and
- Develop appropriate decision support tools, outreach, and training programs for regional and local resource managers.

Budget
The FY 2012 Budget allocated $2.13 million to support biological, chemical, and physical modeling efforts for the National Ocean Acidification Program, as described above in Theme 3 (see Appendix 2 for more details). Agencies presently supporting ocean acidification modeling efforts include NASA, NOAA, NSF, and USGS.

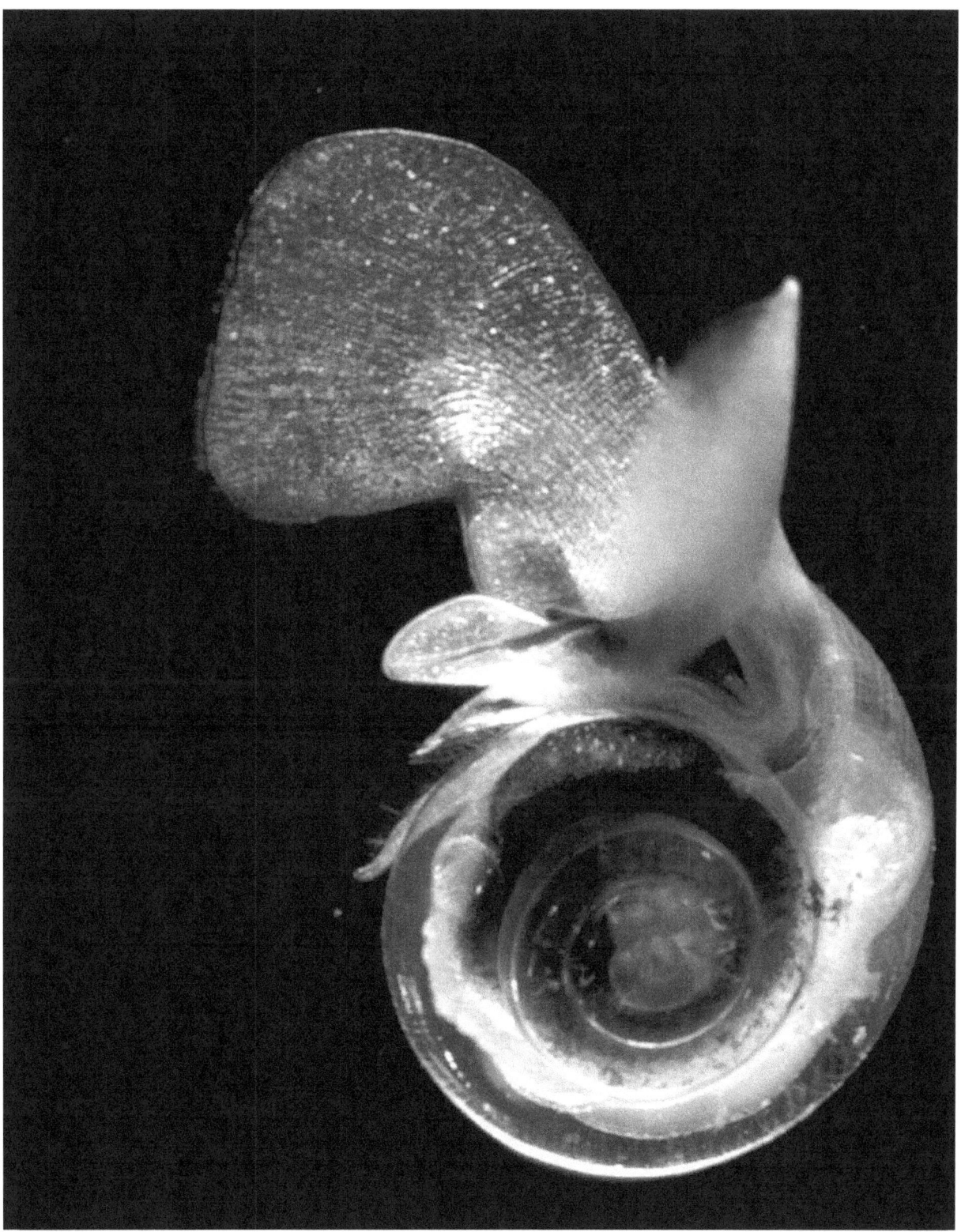

Pteropods, like the one shown here, are an important prey species for many fish in high latitude ecosystems, including Alaskan pink salmon. (Credit: NOAA, PMEL)

Theme 4. Technology Development and Standardization of Measurements

A key component of any scientific program is the ability to measure all of the required parameters while ensuring adequate data quality. This is particularly true for ocean acidification research, which is rapidly developing into a multidisciplinary program with many facets. Additional technologies and methods of standardization are required to meet the needs of other themes in this strategy (see Themes 1 and 2). Careful documentation and archival storage of the measurements is also a fundamental requirement (see Theme 7).

Numerous studies have been performed to qualify and quantify the effects of ocean acidification on marine organisms and ecosystems, but some contradictory conclusions have been reported due to, among other factors, the use of different sampling and experimental protocols. Improved spatial and temporal sampling is needed to increase statistical power and detect biologically meaningful effects; to maximize the likelihood that non-significant results are really a reflection of no biological effect; and to minimize the likelihood that such results are caused by insufficient replication for the levels of variation present in the experimental system (Havenhand and Schlegel 2009). The numerous variables affecting experiment conclusions increase the difficulty of producing reliable results. In many cases, long-term experiments under highly monitored conditions must be performed to correctly attribute changes in organism health to ocean acidification. For example, carbonate chemistry shows significant diurnal and seasonal changes (Kleypas *et al.* 2006), emphasizing the need to incorporate the full dynamic ranges observed in the field (Theme 1) to predict changes due to ocean acidification. Some factors that might affect experimental results are temperature, nutrient availability, light abundance, and distinct individual responses owing to changes in species interaction. Other factors that may result in misleading conclusions are inappropriate experimental protocols such as mis-identification of the experimental unit and pseudoreplication, misinterpretation of data, and inconsistent model parameterization (Hurlbert 1984; Raven *et al.* 2005; Riebesell *et al.* 2010).

A deficiency in most ocean research is specific instrumentation for continuous autonomous monitoring in situ. This holds true specifically for the measurement of inorganic carbon species impacting the ocean biota, but also for the bulk and specific indicators of ecological response. For example, while autonomous measurement capabilities for pH and pCO_2 on buoys and other platforms are commercially available, promising methods for assessing exchanges with the benthos (seafloor) over a range of depths and habitats, are still under development. If the priorities outlined in the previous themes are to be implemented, particularly the establishment of long-term monitoring sites and greatly expanded field research, the availability, affordability, and robustness of autonomous capabilities including in situ sensors, Autonomous Underwater Vehicle (AUV) technologies, and autosamplers will have to be improved and made more accessible.

Requirements and Recommendations

Effective ocean acidification monitoring and research programs require strong technology development and measurement standardization components to improve capabilities for studying the response of organisms to rising CO_2 and changing climate. Critical efforts include: ensuring that appropriate, comparable research protocols are applied; the development, standardization, and implementation of measurement approaches and research methods; sensor and other technology development; and establishment and maintenance of centers of expertise and community research facilities.

Several recent planning documents and workshop reports have promoted the development of standardized approaches and new instrumentation for ocean acidification research (e.g., Kleypas *et al.* 2006; Fabry *et al.* 2008; Borges *et al.* 2010), and this strategic research plan supports use of these recommendations.

- Issues perceived by the scientific community as key to enabling comparability among results include (Orr *et al.* 2009; Riebesell *et al.* 2010):
- Use of appropriate pH measurement protocols and pH scale (recommendations and methods can be found in Riebesell *et al.* 2010, and references therein).

- Use of adequate methods to manipulate and measure carbonate chemistry during experiments (recommendations and methods can be found in Riebesell *et al.* 2010, and references therein).
- New method development for less-expensive and lower sample volume measurements of DIC and TA, as well as for proxies that may indicate stress on marine biota. Use of pCO_2 and pH values in models that reflect realistic levels of ocean acidification relevant for the coming century. Values of pCO_2 exceeding realistic ranges can follow or be coupled with realistic values, but they should not be used as sole-study values.
- Properly maintaining and slowly acclimating organisms to the stressor agent. Protocols to properly maintain sensitive species in the laboratory need to be developed.
- Monitoring all major variables affecting overall organism response to ocean acidification. Environmental factors affecting organism response, such as temperature, light, nutrients, and dissolved oxygen, should be monitored in addition to carbonate system parameters.
- Designing experiments to maximize statistical power. Observations should be reproducible, experiments should be repeated whenever possible, experimental units properly identified, and treatments should be replicated with little chance of confouding.
- Use of statistically informative multivariate techniques might be necessary in experiments that measure multiple response variables.
- Improved autonomous capabilities including: enhanced and new sensors with increased endurance able to measure DIC and/or TA; more reliable autonomous sample collection; and integration into AUV platforms.

Research Protocols

The best methods for discrete and underway measurements of the inorganic carbon system are well established and described in great detail in the Guide to Best Practices for Ocean CO_2 Measurements (Dickson *et al.* 2007; Figure 7). Similarly, the World Ocean Circulation Experiment Manual for hydrographic measurements, including dissolved oxygen and nutrients, was recently updated to reflect the current state of the science6. Other programs have also developed standard methods for various relevant biological measurements. Finally, the European Union project, European Project on Ocean Acidification (EPOCA), has recently published a Guide to Best Practices for Ocean Acidification Research and Data Reporting (Riebesell *et al.* 2010; Figure 7) that builds on the Dickson *et al.* (2007) guide with specific recommendations for ocean acidification studies. Both of these documents were developed and reviewed by a broad international group of scientific experts and should be followed whenever possible.

One significant issue discussed in Riebesell *et al.* (2010) is the importance of making appropriate choices of measurements based on the best "fitness for purpose". This includes not only the choice of which measurements to make, but also a consideration of the acceptable level of uncertainty for measurements in relation to a particular research goal. Thus, the high degree of accuracy and precision required for long-term, open-ocean measurements as outlined by Dickson *et al.* (2007) may be relaxed somewhat in short-term coastal experiments or laboratory studies where these techniques are impractical and the highest precision is not required to address the specific question being asked (Riebesell *et al.* 2010).

Figure 7. Guide to Best Practices for Ocean CO_2 Measurements (Dickson et al. 2007) and Guide to Best Practices for Ocean Acidification Research and Data Reporting (Riebesell et al. 2010).

In addition to the recommendations put forth by these guides, inorganic carbon Certified Reference Materials (CRMs) are available from the laboratory of A. Dickson (Scripps Institution of Oceanography) for verifying that DIC and TA measurements are consistent with an agreed-upon international standard. These verification procedures are essential for ensuring that measurements made by the growing community of ocean acidification researchers are accurate and comparable. Low ionic strength CRMs should be investigated for Great Lake and other fresh water and mesohaline studies. The Dickson Laboratory is also preparing limited quantities of high ionic strength buffers that will be available to help calibrate pH measurements in seawater. Reference materials are also being developed for inorganic nutrients. The use of CRMs is critical for ocean carbon cycle science and will be equally important for ocean acidification research. Funding for the production of these CRMs, work to certify these reference materials for additional carbon parameters, and expanded production of pH buffers must be ensured for the success of the ocean carbon and ocean acidification programs. Steps should be taken to ensure that the CRM program is not reliant upon one investigator who must apply for research funding every few years.

Since there will certainly be many laboratories making chemical measurements as part of their ocean acidification studies, it is important that each laboratory properly documents its procedures for ensuring the accuracy of their measurements. As stated in the best practice guide's chapter on the carbon dioxide system in seawater, "Additional efforts are required to document procedures effectively and to establish a community-wide quality assurance scheme for each technique" (Dickson et al. 2007). Such a scheme will necessitate that each laboratory achieve the following:
- Writing appropriate SOPs for the techniques they are using.
- Using inter-laboratory comparison exercises to assess the various figures of merit for each method (accuracy and precision).
- Regular use of certified reference materials to assist in the quality control.
- Regular laboratory performance testing using blind samples.
- Working collaboratively to ensure that high-quality standards are available to the scientific community.

It should be noted that the ocean acidification best practices are an evolving activity. Thus, financial support for guide updates and methods development/assessment working groups will continue to be essential. A full understanding of ocean acidification will require biological and chemical measurements that include much more than the inorganic carbon system. As relevant measurements are explored and appropriate techniques developed, the community will need to be informed of the latest state-of-the-art in ocean acidification measurement approaches and techniques.

Procedures should be put in place to ensure that proposals funded through the federal ocean acidification programs will follow the guidelines and quality assurance/quality control (QA/QC) procedures discussed above.

Chemical and Biological Measurement Approaches

Oceanographers currently use a variety of tools to observe the ocean. These include satellite observations, shipboard sampling programs, and autonomous in situ instruments. All of these approaches are employed to varying degrees for ocean acidification research (Theme 2). One common aspect of all the ocean acidification research themes is the need to characterize the inorganic carbon system. Methods exist for discrete inorganic carbon measurements from the water column samples, but to properly address the monitoring and experimental needs outlined in this strategic research plan, a variety of approaches, including extensive use of autonomous instruments, will be required. Commercial systems are available for moored measurements of pCO_2 and pH, but this is not an ideal measurement pair as outlined in the following section on technology development (this Theme). A significant investment is needed in additional monitoring technology development to properly assess the full carbon system using unmanned platforms, including moorings, gliders, autonomous vehicles, and floats.

In some cases, existing tools will need to be employed in new environments and modified appropriately. For example, surveys that document the natural variability in near-reef carbonate chemistry are underway but in limited areas (Yates and Halley 2006a, 2006b see also PMEL Coral Reef Moorings). Such surveys are benefited through the use of in situ instruments and high-frequency water samplers as well as small vessel-based water sampling at selected reefs across large latitudinal gradients. Methods have been established for measuring calcification and extension rates from cores of massive reef-building stony (scleractinian) corals (Buddemeier and Kinzie 1976; Chalker and Barnes 1990). These methods need to be applied systematically both to older massive corals and to younger branching and encrusting corals broadly distributed across gradients of aragonite saturation state. In addition, a global array of simple calcification plates (or similar devices) should be deployed to monitor the calcification rates of sessile calcareous organisms, such as crustose coralline algae, a major reef builder that often acts as the "cement" holding reefs together. There is also a need to calibrate existing ocean acidification-specific geochemical proxies (e.g., measurements of boron and carbon isotopes) and to develop new multiple proxy techniques to complement these growth and calcification measurements.

In addition to the existing research tools, the development of new approaches to ocean acidification research is needed. For example, the coral reef projects of the Census of Marine Life have developed Autonomous Reef Monitoring Structures (ARMS) as systematic collecting devices, and they are currently developing mass parallel molecular sequencing capabilities to allow comparative and time-series analyses of indices of invertebrate biodiversity for hard-bottom habitats around the globe (Brainard et al. 2009, Box 7). Similar systematic collecting devices should be employed to assess biodiversity changes in soft-bottom and planktonic communities. Other cost-effective tools for monitoring biological shifts in community structure include passive Ecological Acoustic Recorders (Lammers et al. 2008; Sueur et al. 2008). These tools are only applicable if the geochemical composition of the sampled water body is well-characterized and monitored over time, so it is important to ensure that both the biology and geochemistry are monitored together.

Changes in the trophic balance of ecosystems can also be discerned by variation in the photosynthesis-to-respiration ratio, which can be observed using continuous dissolved oxygen measurements (Silverman et al. 2007). For critical regions, such as high latitudes and coastal areas, abundances and distributions of key taxa should be tracked with sufficient precision and resolution to detect possible shifts in relation to the changes in the geochemical parameters. There is an immediate need for such data on calcifying organisms in regions that are projected to become under-saturated with respect to aragonite in the coming decades. Rapid, cost-effective technologies for quantifying abundances of targeted organisms should be a central component of an integrated ocean acidification observation network.

Box 7. Examples of Novel Approches to In Situ Research

Autonomous Reef Monitoring Structures

The Census of Coral Reef Ecosystems (CReefs), project was established in 2006 as the coral reef component of the Census of Marine Life (CoML), a 10-year (2000-2010) international effort to examine the global diversity, distribution, and abundance of marine life. CReefs collaborators from Scripps Institution of Oceanography, the Australian Institute of Marine Science, and the NOAA Pacific Islands Fisheries Science Center (PIFSC) Coral Reef Ecosystem Division (CRED) developed Autonomous Reef Monitoring Structures (ARMS) as a tool for monitoring the invertebrate biodiversity of coral reefs. The ARMS design was intended to be relatively inexpensive, easy to build, and rugged enough for deployment into varying oceanic conditions (Brainard et al. 2009). An ARMS is comprised of alternating open and semi-enclosed layers that provide habitat for invertebrates after it is deployed on a coral reef. ARMS units are ultimately retrieved for analysis, and invertebrate species are then identified visually and/or using genetic techniques.

Submersible Habitat for Analyzing Reef Quality

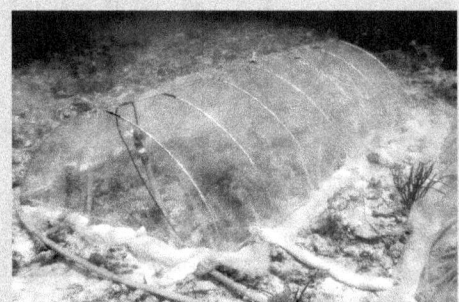

Monitoring and experimentation are required to understand the cause-and-effect relationships relatedto biological and chemical processes (Yates and Halley 2003), including those related to ocean acidification. The Submersible Habitat for Analyzing Reef Quality (SHARQ) is a large, portable incubation chamber designed by USGS researchers to isolate a mass of water over the underlying substrate. A flow-through analytical system enables continuous, 24-hour monitoring of water chemistry resulting from seafloor community processes (e.g., photosynthesis, respiration, and calcification).Collection of 24-hour monitoring data enables geographic comparison of reefs in terms of system functionality, and SHARQ could be used to compare effects of ocean acidification among global reef systems and other carbonate-dependent habitats. Additionally, SHARQ may be an appropriate platform for conducting in situ manipulative experiments to further explore laboratory results (Theme 2)

Technology Development

There is an immediate need to develop autonomous, commercial analytical systems for high frequency measurements of DIC and TA on a variety of surface platforms. Robust, low-power, inexpensive sensors also need to be developed for other autonomous subsurface platforms that are becoming available to the scientific community. Although currently there are no carbonate system sensors ready for profiling floats, the addition of commercially available oxygen sensors to the nascent or existing international monitoring programs, such as the Argo Program, would help constrain carbon distributions through empirical relationships (e.g., Juranek et al. 2009) as well as directly evaluating biogeochemical changes in the ocean. There is a critical need for intensive time-series measurements from sensors and other analytical devices on moored buoys in high productivity coastal and estuarine systems, as CO_2 and carbonate ion concentrations in these waters can vary substantially on timescales from hours to decades due to tides, photosynthesis and respiration, and/or fresh water inputs. Variations in calcium concentrations in these systems also affect the solubility of calcium carbonate minerals produced by mollusks (e.g., clams, oysters, and snails) and other ecologically or commercially important marine organisms. Calcium and magnesium may also vary non-conservatively in estuaries further complicating interpretations of mineral solubility in these waters. New technologies are essential to meeting these needs. To constrain the inorganic carbon parameters to the precision and accuracy necessary to assess spatial and temporal variability of ocean acidification and its impacts, TA and/or DIC measurement capabilities are required. Additionally, improved programs are needed that will attract a larger range of potential business partners and encourage significantly faster commercialization of new instruments (see Prevention, Control, and Mitigation of Harmful Algal Blooms program as a model9).

California Current Ecosystem Buoy, Credit: PMEL

Although promising developmental efforts are underway, they require continued resources and field testing. Field deployments and transitioning of instrumentation from research labs to viable commercial production are often lacking in funded development efforts. In addition to new instrumentation for laboratory, ship, and buoy settings, the adaptation of novel platforms such as gliders, AUVs, drifters, and autonomous surface vehicles to accommodate sensors for ocean acidification research is also desired. These efforts could benefit from a coordinated Federal approach using existing mechanisms such as the National Oceanographic Partnership Program and the NOAA Alliance for Coastal Technologies program (e.g., 2012 Technology Evaluation), as well as agency efforts such as NSF's Oceanographic Technology and Interdisciplinary Coordination program or the Federal Small Business Innovation Research programs.

Centers of Expertise and Community Research Facilities

The current analytical capacities and expertise in carbon system dynamics, as it pertains to ocean acidification, are not sufficient in most labs. Fortunately, several research labs (including some listed in Theme 1, as well as NOAA's Pacific Marine Environmental Laboratory) have acquired personnel with appropriate expertise and instrumentation to perform key measurements for ocean acidification as part of their decades-long involvement in global ocean CO_2 programs. Geographic expansion in the number of these centers, which can be located in both federal and academic laboratories, will help make them more accessible and allow them to develop expertise in the ecosystem structure and issues unique to different regions. It is not practical for these labs to make all or even most of the carbon system measurements for a national ocean acidification program, but they can provide some analytical services, lead efforts to continue best practices, conduct round-robin quality assurance studies (i.e., sending samples for labs to analyze as unknowns), and train personnel in proper protocols and analysis. They can also advise in the design of perturbation studies to predict responses of organisms to future anticipated CO_2 levels. These services will require specific support, but will benefit the entire ocean acidification community.

The OCB Program, funded jointly by NSF, NASA, and NOAA, held an ocean acidification short course, taught by experts in the field, to educate the broader community on available techniques, proper analytical methods, and potential pitfalls in designing ocean acidification studies. Similar training efforts will be needed for the next several years to teach biology to the chemists, chemistry to the biologists, and to educate the new generation of scientists on useful approaches for studying ocean acidification. This capacity-building effort will not only be helpful to scientists, but also to resource managers (e.g., marine sanctuaries, state and local water management groups) and relevant industry representatives (e.g., shellfish industry, instrument manufacturers) that are interested in learning more about ways to understand ocean acidification in their area of interest.

Ocean acidification training courses in different regions and habitats could be tailored to address the particular concerns of that area. Engagement of non-governmental organizations (NGOs) and regional or professional associations for these educational efforts should be encouraged as an avenue for reaching stakeholders (Theme 6). The involvement of local researchers and resource managers can provide the regional perspective, particularly in the ecosystem structure and local needs, to make the training courses more effective.

Some aspects of ocean acidification research (e.g., mesocosm studies and FOCE experiments) can be quite expensive to develop and will require sustained infrastructure support to maintain. The development of a few national facilities for ocean acidification research (refer to Box 2 for examples of existing and proposed facilities) in different environments should enable more-efficient use of resources and ultimately result in higher quality research. For example, a large mesocosm facility that is available to ocean acidification researchers would allow a series of high-quality, proposal-based, and peer-reviewed studies to be performed without each individual investigator having to duplicate efforts and build new facilities from scratch. The availability of instrumentation to make basic measurements (e.g., high quality carbon measurements) would also allow better comparability between different studies performed at the facility. It is critical, as with global observations, to coordinate these national facilities with those of neighboring countries such as Canada and Mexico.

Goals
Ocean acidification measurement technologies will evolve dramatically over the next decade, and most of the goals listed below are already receiving some investment. The short-term goals represent recommended priorities if funding becomes available. The long-term goals also represent recommended priorities, but they may take longer to yield their full benefits and/or require completion of one or more short-term goals. A well-coordinated ocean acidification program will help ensure that advancements in technology are developed systematically and quickly spread through the community.

Short-term (3-5 years)
Some achievable, short-term goals that will address the most pressing current deficiencies are (Orr et al. 2009; NRC 2010a):
- Develop standardized methodology for measurement (Theme 2) of critical biological parameters specific to biological response to ocean acidification (as identified by efforts conducted under Theme 1).
- Establish validated SOPs for all geochemical parameter measurements (Themes 1 and 2). Results obtained under distinct validated protocols should be comparable.
- Ensure cross-calibration of measurement techniques.
- Develop best practices for manipulative field experiments and for studies in natural CO_2 venting sites and low pH regions (Theme 1).
- Establish a domestic and international network of ocean acidification research and monitoring groups that work together to develop new approaches for ocean acidification research (in conjunction with efforts described in Theme 6).
- Develop a program to ensure that researchers are following consistent and appropriate analytical methods with documented QA/QC procedures.
- Enhance programs that foster development and deployment of new sensor technologies needed for ocean acidification research.
- Expand inorganic CRM development and production efforts to better support the growing ocean acidification program needs.
- Facilitate the transition of newly developed technologies from research to commercial development.

- Calibrate existing and develop new geochemical proxies to facilitate paleo-oceanographic studies of organismal and ecosystem response to ocean acidification (Theme 1).

Long-term (10 years)
The following should be achievable within 10 years with adequate funding:
- Develop and commercialize instrumentation and techniques to improve capability to measure chemical (with special focus on DIC and TA) and biological variables over space and time, including affordable autonomous sensors, more accessible and affordable high-quality instrumentation, new remote sensing, and in situ technologies.
- Integrate existing and new instruments for conducting carbon and biological system analyses onto a variety of platforms including autonomous surface and subsurface vehicles.
- Establish 2-4 regional centers of expertise providing routine analytical services and analytical training for the community and with infrastructure that is available for the community to come and conduct specific research studies.

These goals and priorities are likely to evolve over the next decade and as specific implementation plans are developed, but should provide a first-cut at the minimum level of support required to develop the ocean acidification program envisioned with this strategy.

Budget
The FY 2012 Budget allocated $612,000 to support the technology development and measurement standardization efforts of the National Ocean Acidification Program (see Appendix 2 for more details). Agencies presently supporting ocean acidification technology development and measurement standardization efforts include NOAA, NSF, and USGS.

Theme 5. Assessment of Socioeconomic Impacts and Development of Strategies to Conserve Marine Organisms and Ecosystems

Coastal and marine environments are intricately linked with the human cultural and social systems and the economic markets that have drawn on those resources to foster prosperity. Socioeconomics is the study of those human dimensions; it encompasses the interactions of society with its surroundings and the economic and social effects of choices made within society. Beyond examining the alterations in ocean chemistry that will result from increased atmospheric CO_2 concentrations and the subsequent impacts on marine life, we must recognize the dependence of society on that changing marine environment and the consequences of those changes to society. The National Ocean Policy recognizes the importance of valuing ecosystems, which include the human environment and identifies ecosystem-based management as a foundation of responsible ocean stewardship.

From an economic perspective, the ocean and coastal environment provide valuable goods and services. The "goods" refer to humans' consumptive use of marine resources and include crustaceans, mollusks, fish, and other organisms and items that we harvest for food and other consumer products. Some of the "services" include the cycling of carbon, maintaining biodiversity, and providing means for recreation. The human activities that rely on these goods and services are often intertwined with the social fabric of coastal communities and tribal groups. For example, commercial fishing provides income to a household, but for many such households it is also a way of life that is intertwined with how households operate, how spouses share responsibilities and generations interact, how communities are organized, and how people within those communities see their interactions with each other and the natural world. Such is the case for many people that reside, work, and recreate along our coasts.

To Washington's tribal communities, ocean acidification is both a natural resource issue and a significant challenge to their continued identity and cultural survival. With salmon populations just a fraction of their former abundance, tribal fishers depend more and more on the various shellfish species to support their families; almost all of the commercial wild and cultured clam and oyster fisheries in Puget Sound are tribal. The tribes also harvest wild shellfish for ceremonial and subsistence purposes. Negative effects of ocean acidification on the food-web, such as the zooplankton (including pteropods) eaten by salmon, further threaten the ability of tribes to obtain sufficient traditional foods.

We are just beginning to unravel the full effects of increased carbon dioxide in the atmosphere and the resultant alterations in ocean chemistry and, therefore, are not yet in a position to fully understand the consequences that this process will have on our society; however, we can begin to address what range of future outcomes is possible. We know that a decrease in pH can have negative effects on some of those species dependent on calcium carbonate for building their shells or skeletons. Some of these species are directly consumed by humans, while others are part of the food web and would have dietary implications for other economically and culturally important species. A key question is: How fast will these changes occur and to what extent are humans and the affected species able to adapt? Increasing our understanding of the effects of ocean acidification will inform discussions of climate change mitigation and adaptation, thus helping stakeholders and decision makers to respond more efficiently. Put simply, studying the cultural and economic implications of ocean acidification requires an examination of the affected populations, the timing and magnitude of the impacts, and potential responses to reduce the societal damages (NRC 2010a).

As we move forward with studying changes in the environment as a result of ocean acidification, an examination of the cultural and economic aspects must be pursued concurrently. Determining which of the physical effects are likely to have the largest socioeconomic impacts will be useful in guiding research resources to their most efficient use and will aid in developing an adaptation and mitigation strategy. Moore (2011) examines the effects of ocean acidification on the U.S. mollusk fishery and proposes an economic methodology for evaluating the economic effects on finfish and coral reefs. His work could be used to identify areas for additional research in ocean acidification which in turn, could be used to improve the economic predictions.

At this time, there are only a few evaluations of the economic and cultural effects from ocean acidification on which this strategic plan can build. An initial evaluation of the economic consequences on commercial aquaculture and harvest of mollusks in the U.S. estimates revenue declines, job losses, and some indirect economic effects (Cooley and Doney 2009). The economic consequences on shellfish production globally were evaluated by Narita et al. (2012) with estimates of a loss of $6 billion annually, mostly affecting China. The economic impact of the loss of coral reef habitats due to ocean acidification has also been estimated (Brander et al. 2009). As the authors of these studies point out, a robust evaluation of the implications to society is difficult because of the uncertainty surrounding the physical impacts of ocean acidification and how humans would respond. One method for identifying and prioritizing the direction of ocean acidification research in the context of socioeconomic implications is the application of a value of information study similar to that conducted by Costello et al. (1998).

Requirements and Recommendations

Evidenced by the lack of peer-reviewed studies on the socioeconomic impacts of ocean acidification, the current need for research in this area is vast and the directions are many. To some extent, cultural and economic research must follow research in the natural sciences; however, this should not preclude making resources available for evaluation of socioeconomic impacts while still actively supporting research in the natural sciences. Ideally, findings in one area would guide new research in the other. For example, it would be wise for natural scientists to research impacts of ocean acidification on species that are economically and culturally significant. Similarly, social scientists should study impacts that can be accurately represented with models of the biophysical system and are feasibly quantifiable. As such, communication between physical and social scientists, stakeholders, and decision makers will be critical. What follows is a list of research areas that will improve our ability to assess and mitigate the socioeconomic impacts of ocean acidification.

Inventory of Impacts

As our ability to monitor and forecast the physical impacts of ocean acidification improves, we will also be able to improve our assessment of the cultural and economic effects. The NRC (2010a) identified three key areas or sectors where the effects of ocean acidification are most likely to occur based on the current state of knowledge:

- Marine Fisheries – Impacts to commercially valuable finfish will most likely occur through the food web. A reduction or trophic change in planktonic species may reduce the abundance of commercial species since plankton is often a food source and the link between external energy and nutrient sources (light and inorganic chemical species) and higher trophic levels. Alternately, ocean acidification may affect the critical habitat for some species, such as alterations in coral and oyster reefs.
- Aquaculture – Successful hatcheries and grow-out facilities are dependent on careful control of the environment in which their stocks are grown. For saltwater species, ocean water is often pumped in and circulated as opposed to using artificial mixes. A change in the water chemistry, such as a reduction in pH, may result in less productivity of the brood stock and/or may cause high larval mortality. This was evidenced by a recent larval disease outbreak in West coast oyster hatcheries caused by upwelling, low pH water, which provided an advantage to a disease-causing bacterium, *Vibrio tubiashii*. Aquaculturists are interested in the probability, frequency, magnitude, and timing of the changes in water chemistry so they can respond accordingly.
- Tropical Coral Reef Systems – Coral reef systems are complex and already being damaged by other anthropogenic stressors like water pollution, destructive fishing practices, and climate change. The impacts of ocean acidification on the health of corals and coralline algae will exacerbate these already clear impacts. Coral reefs provide habitat for commercial and subsistence fisheries, support tourism and recreation markets, and contribute to marine biodiversity.

Identifying Stakeholder Groups

Identifying stakeholders (business owners, coastal communities, seafood and tourism industries, tribes, etc.)

is a critical step in forming a research agenda and one that requires attention throughout the decision-making process. While ocean acidification is a global issue, many of the economic and cultural effects will be regional and locally specific. Mitigation and adaptation strategies may require inclusion of stakeholders that are part of the solution, such as energy and cement industries and the agricultural community. As data availability and modeling capabilities improve, new stakeholders may emerge. The establishment of a National Program Office for ocean acidification will assist in ensuring the engagement of stakeholders. Additional means of exchanging stakeholders is discussed under Theme 6.

Economic Impact Assessment

Once the effects of ocean acidification have been identified, they should be quantified and, to the extent possible, monetized. Determining the magnitude of a given impact is important information and can be useful when evaluating policy or allocating resources. Expressing those magnitudes in monetary terms can, if done accurately, provide more useful information because the value of mitigating and adapting to some impacts can be compared directly with the costs of achieving those goals. Assessing the economic impacts of ocean acidification will require several components, including long-term forecasts of socioeconomic conditions, valuation of market and non-market impacts (Box 8), integrated assessment modeling (Box 6), social discounting, and uncertainty analysis. Such an impact assessment would then permit analysis of the cost-effectiveness of mitigation and adaptation strategies.

Box 8. Non-market valuation

When policy decisions affect goods and services traded in normal markets, changes in prices and incomes provide a monetary measure of the impact on social welfare. However, it is often the case that goods and services that are not traded in normal markets, but nevertheless contribute to social welfare, are also affected by policy decisions. In these cases, an accurate assessment of economic efficiency requires non-market valuation. There is a wide variety of approaches to non-market valuation, but all of them can be classified as either revealed preference or stated preference. Revealed preference methods rely on observing behavior that is complementary to the non-market good being valued. For example, it is possible to infer a value for the quality of an outdoor recreation site by observing how far people are willing to travel to get there compared with alternative sites. Stated preference methods can provide value estimates when it is too expensive or simply impossible to observe complementary behavior. Stated preference methods rely on surveys containing hypothetical choices that reveal the value that people place on non-market goods and services. While placing monetary values on environmental amenities and ecosystem services is not without controversy, without these monetary measures, it is likely that valuable goods and services will instead be assigned zero value and ignored in policy discussions.

The social cost of carbon (SCC) is a measure of the economic benefit from a marginal reduction in CO_2 emissions and is used to evaluate the economic efficiency of regulations affecting CO_2 emissions (Box 9). All estimates of the SCC produced to date quantify damages from climate change but omit impacts from ocean acidification. This is a potentially large omission that leads to an underestimate of the SCC and the benefits from regulations that reduce CO_2 emissions. In order to more accurately evaluate the economic efficiency of CO_2 emissions policies, the economic losses resulting from ocean acidification must be considered alongside those of climate change.

Aggregate measures of economic impacts, such as percentage Gross Domestic Product lost due to environmental damages, are useful summary statistics but tell only part of the story. It is also important to examine how those impacts are distributed across the affected population. There are a number of dimensions to consider when conducting distributional impacts analyses. Economic impacts of environmental damages can disproportionately affect some state, local, or tribal governments; geographic locations; or subpopulations of interest including historically disadvantaged communities. While economic impact assessments are valuable tools to inform priorities, it should be noted that some values cannot be accurately monetized. Decision makers will require this knowledge as they craft mitigation and adaptation strategies for ocean acidification.

Box 9. Interagency Working Group on Social Cost of Carbon (IWG-SCC)

In 2009, an interagency work group, led by the Council of Economic Advisors, convened with the purpose of providing a consistent set of SCC values for all executive agencies to use in economic analyses of regulations that affect CO_2 emissions. The effort relied heavily on three separate climate integrated assessment models (IAMs): FUND (Tol 2002); DICE (Nordhaus 2008); and PAGE (Hope 2006). The interagency group outlined a set of model inputs to be used in the calculations, including a range of social discount rates; a set of several long-term forecasts for population, income, and greenhouse gas emissions; and the sensitivity of the climate system to atmospheric CO_2 concentrations. Based on these inputs, the three climate IAMs were used to develop a range of SCC estimates. The technical support document for the interagency effort presents the results and a detailed accounting of the methods and assumptions.

Mitigation of Impacts

The most direct way to reduce ocean acidification is to reduce the atmospheric concentration of CO_2. This requires sharp reductions in CO_2 emissions, increasing CO_2 sequestration, or both. Strategies to reduce greenhouse gas emissions have been extensively investigated under climate change discussions and can be found in various reports (e.g., EPA 2005; EPA 2006; Metz et a l. 2007). They include establishment of regulatory standards on emission levels, financial incentives for innovative technology development, tradable permits, increasing energy efficiency, reduction of deforestation, promotion of reforestation, and shifting energy sources from fossil fuels to alternative energy sources. These solutions would require an organized and committed international effort that crosses social, cultural, and political boundaries.

An alternate mitigation strategy is to reduce other marine stressors that exacerbate the impacts of ocean acidification. Coral reefs, for example, face a number of threats other than ocean acidification. Urban and agricultural runoff, sedimentation, and destructive fishing practices also threaten the long-term survival of coral reefs. Reducing other stressors to coral reefs may mitigate the cumulative impact and increase the chances for sustainable coral ecosystems; however, alternate mitigation strategies may not be available for all ocean acidification impacts and those that are will likely be of limited benefit.

Established long-term monitoring and research sites (Themes 1 and 2; Box 2), such as marine protected areas (MPAs) or LTERs (Box 3), should be utilized to test and monitor the efficacy and impacts of chosen ocean acidification mitigation measures. Existing partnerships between Federal agencies and other entities, such as the Department of the Interior's (DOI) Landscape Conservation Cooperatives (LCCs; Box 10), should be drawn upon to develop, test, and evaluate mitigation, as well as adaptation protocols (next section, this Theme) and ensure that they are appropriate for both the environmental and cultural needs of a community or region.

Box 10. Partnerships

Landscape Conservation Cooperatives

The U.S. Fish and Wildlife Service (FWS) and the U.S. Geological Survey (USGS) are working with a diverse group of partners to develop a national network of Landscape Conservation Cooperatives (LCCs). LCCs are applied conservation science partnerships composed of Federal agencies, states, tribes, non-governmental organizations, universities, and stakeholders within geographically defined areas. The goal of the LCCs is to provide a clear focus on climate change modeling and adaptive conservation design with solid management decision-support tools and evaluation of resource monitoring data. They will provide resource managers with adaptive conservation strategies and actions that will anticipate changes in habitat and the abundance and distribution of species.

Pacific Islands Climate Change Cooperative

The Pacific Islands Climate Change Cooperative (PICCC)13, the LCC for the U.S. central Pacific, is a self-directed, non-regulatory conservation alliance whose purpose is to assist those who manage native species, island ecosystems, and key cultural resources in adapting their management to climate change for the continuing benefit of the people of the Pacific Islands. The PICCC provides scientific and technical support for landscape-scale conservation in an adaptive management framework by supporting biological planning, conservation design in a cultural context, prioritization and coordination of research, and inventory and monitoring design.   The PICCC currently include 30 members from Federal, State, private, indigenous, and non-governmental conservation organizations and academic institutions acting in partnership to fulfill the cooperative's mission, vision, and goals. In 2010, PICCC funded a series of projects that will vastly improve our understanding of how global climate change is manifesting at regional and site-specific scales.

Adaptation Strategies

Some degree of further ocean acidification is inevitable regardless of how effective mitigation efforts are. Adapting to or coping with the resulting impacts will become necessary for some parts of the population and sectors of the economy. Adaptation to changing environmental conditions is not a new concept. Creating crops that are resistant to drought, disease, and pests is one example of a human system adapting to adverse environmental conditions; however, the changes we are likely to see in atmospheric and ocean chemistry present a challenge on a larger scale. An early example of adaptation to ocean acidification is the response of shellfish growers along the Pacific Coast. In recent years, several oyster hatcheries have experienced a near-complete collapse of production. A partnership between industry, academia and federal scientists led to the discovery that high CO_2 (and a resulting low mineral saturation state) in the hatchery waters was causing the decline. As a result, hatcheries are now monitoring water quality conditions very closely and have developed adaptation strategies including closing the intake valves to the hatcheries when corrosive waters are detected and other manipulations of the chemistry to reduce its corrosiveness before it reaches the growing oysters. Other adaptive strategies may include breeding programs that support stocks of oysters that are genetically able to adapt (see Ocean Margin Ecosystems Group for Acidification Studies for more information). Adaptation is a risk-management strategy that has costs and is not foolproof. The effectiveness of any specific adaptation requires consideration of the expected value of the avoided damages against the costs of implementing the adaptation strategy (Easterling et al. 2004; Metz et al. 2007). Additionally, ocean acidification adaptation strategies should, if possible, compliment strategies developed for other climate and ecosystem stressors (e.g., NOAA 2010b).

Goals

Assessments of the socioeconomic impacts of ocean acidification are essential for developing appropriate adaptation and conservation strategies; however, socioeconomic components have typically been lacking in past ocean acidification studies, and few of the goals listed below are receiving much, if any, attention. The short-term goals represent recommended priorities if funding becomes available. The long-term goals also represent recommended priorities, but they may take longer to yield their full benefits and/or require completion of one or more short-term goals.

Short-term (3-5 years)

- Support inclusion of cultural and economic components in studies of the effects of ocean acidification, where appropriate.
- Encourage marine policy programs to incorporate ocean acidification and its cultural and economic impacts into their curricula and areas of study.
- Foster communication and collaboration between natural and social scientists as well as training about the issue of ocean acidification to ensure that all researchers studying the impacts of ocean acidification are working with state-of-the-science methods and the most accurate data available.
- Conduct non-market valuation studies to estimate damages from anticipated impacts of ocean acidification.
- Develop integrated models that link physical, biological, and economic systems in order to estimate the economic and distributional impacts of ocean acidification.
- Encourage Federal agencies to include consideration of ocean acidification as part of their National Environmental Policy Act process.

Long-term (10 years)

- Foster communication between researchers, stakeholders, and decision makers to develop efficient mitigation and adaptation strategies (in conjunction with efforts described in Theme 6).
- Develop decision support tools to assist national, state, and local governments in developing management options and understanding their implications.
- Provide businesses and communities that will be adversely affected by ocean acidification with the information they need to develop adaptation action plans (Theme 6).
- Develop metrics to test the efficacy of adaptation and mitigation strategies.

Budget

The FY 2012 Budget allocated $92,000 to support socioeconomic assessments and development of conservation strategies under the National Ocean Acidification Program (see Appendix 2 for more details). Only NOAA presently supports socioeconomic research related to ocean acidification.

Theme 6. Education, Outreach, and Engagement Strategy on Ocean Acidification

The FOARAM Act requires an "Ocean Acidification Information Exchange" that would "go beyond chemical and biological measurements alone, to produce syntheses and assessments that would be accessible to and understandable by managers, policy makers, and the general public. This is an important priority for decision support, but it will require specific resources and expertise, particularly in science communication, to operate effectively" (NRC 2010a).

Progress on an ocean acidification implementation plan hinges on garnering support from key stakeholder groups. That support requires an understanding of ocean acidification that can be achieved by outreach and engagement. A report of the Ocean Acidification Task Force (OATF) recognizes both the importance and challenge of effective public outreach, stating, "Indeed, there is growing evidence that the interest in, and appreciation for, science in the United States is extremely low. If we expect our Federal legislators to provide substantive long-term support, the IWG-OA will need to consider how they can effectively improve communication about ocean acidification research and its relevance to society" (ORRAP 2010).

Requirements and Recommendations

As described in a recent NRC report Informing an Effective Response to Climate Change, "the nation lacks comprehensive, robust, and credible information systems to inform climate choices and evaluate their effectiveness" (NRC 2010b). Stemming from this same lack of information is a need for greater public education, outreach, and engagement on ocean acidification and its causes. The Interagency Ocean Policy Task Force (OPTF) established, as one of the National Priority Objectives, a need for public education on ocean acidification through formal and informal programs (OPTF 2010). By extension, an outreach and education component of the National Ocean Acidification Program that effectively informs and engages stakeholders and the general public will constitute an important component of domestic policy.

Recognizing the needs mentioned above, the OATF recommends that Federal agencies dedicate significant resources to the development of a robust and effective ocean acidification outreach effort, using domestic and international NGO, academic, government, and donor communities to foster this process. A well-funded strategy on ocean acidification will ideally address the need for and facilitation of communication and outreach, partnerships with domestic and international NGOs, and other stakeholder groups, and coordination of scientific research and dissemination of scientific information.

The main focus of the education and outreach program should be to enhance ocean acidification literacy by creating educational opportunities that engage stakeholders in an interdisciplinary and international approach to addressing ocean acidification. Secondly, the program should channel resources into coordinating activities among nations and international bodies while building support for U.S. and international ocean acidification programs. An education and outreach program should serve immediate as well as future needs, yet be able to address unforeseen needs by remaining flexible in its outreach message, educational approach, and partnerships.

Ocean acidification is a high priority issue with local effects but global causes. Therefore, education and outreach should have both national and international components. In particular, efforts should focus on regions and communities with greater vulnerability to ocean acidification (e.g., polar regions and regions with a high dependency on coral reef and estuarine fisheries or tourism), because the U.S. has a significant interest in assisting understanding of and response to ocean acidification. In addition to geographic-focused efforts, our outreach and education efforts should engage the broader public, as well as policymakers, such as the United States Congress, and relevant decision-makers at the state and local levels. Such general education efforts will endeavor to incorporate information on the socioeconomic consequences of ocean acidification, along with basic information about ocean acidification and its causes. Moreover, given that communication difficulties may arise more-readily with international stakeholders, education and outreach efforts must make a concerted effort to engage an international audience.

Education and Outreach Activities

The National Ocean Acidification Program Office should take responsibility for the following education and outreach activities:

- Coordinating the design, implementation, and updates of the strategic plan for education and outreach.
- Organizing and hosting education and outreach events, both domestic and international.
- Making scientific assessments available to managers, policy makers, and the general public as useful education tools.
- Preparing materials for education and outreach events and any subsequent reports, updates, and/or publicity associated with those events.
- Developing a list of feedback metrics to measure the effectiveness of education and outreach campaigns on ocean acidification and arranging for independent reviews of the effectiveness of education and outreach activities.
- Serving as a central hub for a broad range of ocean acidification resources, including Federal non-federal, national, and international tools.
- Identifying opportunities for partnerships between U.S. agencies, international governments, NGOs, academia, and industry, including opportunities for funding.
- Producing materials on ocean acidification that are appropriate for media outlets and developing a media resource webpage to be hosted on the Program Office's website.
- Representing the U.S education and outreach efforts at domestic and international meetings and conferences on ocean acidification.
- Designing and maintaining an education and outreach web portal.
- Providing linkages between researchers and students for structured, sustained, and meaningful educational opportunities.
- Coordinating investment on ocean acidification education efforts and initiatives across the federal government, helping achieve a coherent and purposeful set of products, resources, and services.
- Utilizing existing outreach and education networks, such as the Cooperative Extension System, which has offices in every county in the U.S., and state Sea Grant Marine Advisory Service offices, which focus on coastal states. These networks have trained professionals with expertise in the development and delivery of science-based educational programs to the general public.

Web Portal

The Ocean Acidification Information Exchange mandated by the FOARAM Act is required to "make information on ocean acidification developed through or utilized by the interagency ocean acidification program accessible through electronic means, including information which would be useful to policymakers, researchers, and other stakeholders in mitigating or adapting to the impacts of ocean acidification", a task that will require the creation and maintenance of an education and outreach web portal maintained by the National Ocean Acidification Program Office (see Theme 7 for details on the complementary data access portal). In an effort to support use of this portal by non-English speakers and an international audience, the web portal can be a gateway to information posted in multiple languages. Key education and outreach resources and services that could be provided through a web portal include:

- Education and outreach materials on ocean acidification science and implications, including interactive web-based education tools, literature (e.g., scientific publications, press releases, and newspaper and magazine articles), and links to existing tools.
- Updates and summaries on the latest science on ocean acidification.
- Interactive dialogue among stakeholders, the National Program Office, and world experts on ocean acidification.
- Ongoing domestic and international research on ocean acidification.
- Data services and products based on the complete suite of Federal, State, local, and international ocean acidification research and monitoring efforts (see Theme 7).
- Ocean acidification outreach and educational activities, such as domestic and international conferences,

meetings, webinars, films, lectures, and podcasts.
- Educational courses and workshops on ocean acidification for various age groups (young and adult learning) and professionals (e.g., educators, NGOs, and government employees).
- Funding opportunities for governmental and non-governmental activities regarding ocean acidification including research, education, and outreach.

Engaging Stakeholders

Actively engaging ocean acidification stakeholders in the education and outreach activities will ensure better long-term success of other components of the national strategy. There are numerous stakeholder groups that will be affected by ocean acidification. Identification of key groups (Theme 5) will help focus education and outreach efforts. For example, interests for the domestic and international engagement strategies in ocean acidification are held by, but not limited to, NGOs; the fisheries, aquaculture, and seafood industries; recreational fishing and diving sectors; natural resource managers; and coastal tribes and territories.

Broadly, education and outreach will target interest groups who contribute to ocean acidification, those being impacted by ocean acidification, and those who can help to mitigate or adapt the effects of ocean acidification. In particular, populations that live in regions where oceans are particularly sensitive to ocean acidification may require more immediate engagement. Successful education and outreach activities also benefit from the support of those who generate the information being disseminated; involvement of scientists and NGOs will help to maintain consistent messages and efficient use of funds. Education and outreach programs should not take a limited view of stakeholder groups; audiences for engagement should include those whose future participation will be needed when anticipated changes in ocean acidification policy take place.

Engagement activities should involve a wide array of educational opportunities that encourage interdisciplinary understanding of the impacts of ocean acidification and be open to international participation and new education and outreach opportunities when feasible.

Venues for engaging and interacting with ocean acidification education and outreach include, but are not limited to: professional and scientific meetings, workshops, policy institutes ("think tanks"), aquaria and museums, schools and universities, scientific and non-scientific publications, and the media (e.g., television, popular literature, radio, newspapers, and virtual social networking platforms). The National Ocean Acidification Program Office will take advantage of ongoing activities such as these, but, when more appropriate, should initiate engagement activities with the overall objective of education, outreach, or coordination.

Engagement of stakeholders in ocean acidification education and outreach will help to address OATF's recognized critical need for increased "collaboration between the various stakeholders." The National Ocean Acidification Program Office should coordinate efforts between NGOs, donors, government agencies, international entities, and other participants in education and outreach activities. Collaboration will benefit from the work already being done by NGOs and the fishing and aquaculture industries in their efforts to understand and communicate sustainability (ORRAP 2010). Moreover, engagement will benefit from being linked to ongoing education and outreach programs already underway by Federal and state agencies, NGOs, and the international community.

Linking to Existing Programs and Organizations

The National Ocean Acidification Program Office should take advantage of ongoing education and outreach activities (refer to Box 11 for examples). These ongoing activities include the range of initiatives on ocean acidification education programs as well as those related to marine sciences, general science, and climate change. In addition, the range of partners should include the full array of ongoing initiatives by the U.S. government, NGOs, international organizations, and other stakeholder groups when feasible.

Within the U.S. government, education and outreach materials are made available by NOAA, USGS, NSF, NASA, EPA, FWS, USDA, and National Park Service concerning climate change. Initiatives such as these could expand to address ocean acidification, if they have not already, through active engagement by the ocean acidification community. The National Ocean Acidification Program should also work in partnership with the National Ocean Council (NOC) Subcommittee on Education as ocean acidification science is closely related to several of the NOC priority objectives (such as "Ocean Economy," "Coastal and Ocean Resilience," and "Local Choices").

The international component of an education and outreach engagement strategy, in particular, will benefit from linkages to established international collaborations, agreements, and organizations. These avenues include international NGOs, scientific collaborations, and non-binding agreements. The U.S. is an active participant in the leading international scientific collaboration on ocean acidification research. International science collaborations such as these, as well as official science and technology agreements between the U.S. and foreign governments, can be used to catalyze education and outreach on this environmental issue. Official foreign government collaborations between the U.S. and other nations on ocean acidification research and assessment already include initiatives via the Arctic Council's Arctic Monitoring and Assessment Program working group and the collaborative research cruises with the Canadian government and academia. The U.S. will also participate in the Ocean Acidification International Coordination Centre, an international partnership that will serve as a mechanism for scientists to further collaborate on this pressing issue.

Box 11. Examples of programs and organizations with existing education and outreach initiatives and venues for ocean acidification or greater climate change issues.

U.S. government-led initiatives (Refer to Appendix 1 for detailed information regarding ongoing U.S. government initiatives):
- Multilateral partnerships (land-based pollution and marine debris)
- Coastal America
- Coral Reef Task Force
- Biomass Research and Development Board
- U.S. Global Change Research Program (USGCRP)

U.S. government-academia partnerships:
- American Society of Limnology and Oceanography (ASLO)
- Centers for Ocean Sciences Education Excellence (COSEE)
- Climate Change Education Partnership (CCEP)
- Climate Literacy and Energy Awareness Network (CLEAN) Pathway
- Coopertive Ecosystem Study Units (CESU)
- Integrated Ocean Observing System (IOOS)
- Ocean Carbon and Biogeochemistry Program (OCB)
- National Parks Service Research Learning Centers
- National Estuary Program (NEP)
- Washington State Sea Grant

Other U.S. efforts (States, U.S. NGOs, and other non-governmental initiatives and efforts):
- American Geophysical Union (AGU)
- American Association for the Advancement of Science (AAAS) Conference on Promoting Climate Literacy through Informal Science
- National Academy of Science
- Association of Science - Technology Centers (ASTC)
- California Current Acidification Network (CCAN)
- Environmental Defense Fund
- Gordon and Betty Moore Foundation
- Natural Resources Defense Council (NRDC)
- Ocean Conservancy
- The Nature Conservancy
- The Oceanography Society
- Pew Center

- Association of Zoos and Aquariums (AZA) and public aquaria, museums, and zoos, both U.S. and foreign
- National Marine Educators Association (NMEA)
- National Network of Climate Change Interpreters (NNOCCI)
- Climate Literacy Zoo Education Network (CliZEN)
- Washington State Ocean Acidification Research Center

International NGOs:
- Conservation International
- International Union for the Conservation of Nature
- OCEANA
- World Wildlife Fund

International scientific collaborations:
- Ocean Acidification International Coordination Center
- IPCC working groups on ocean acidification
- International "Oceans in a High CO_2 World" International Meetings
- International Science Advisory Panel for the European Project on Ocean Acidification (EPOCA)
- Joint Integrated Marine Biogeochemistry and Ecosystem Research – Surface Ocean Lower Atmosphere Study (IMBER/SOLAS) working groups

Creating New Partnerships

Beyond linking to existing education and outreach initiatives, the National Ocean Acidification Program Office will have to forge new partnerships. The need for new partnerships will become clear after an assessment of current efforts has highlighted successful strategies and important gaps. New partnerships and initiatives will be streamlined with ongoing efforts as to avoid redundancy and will target education and outreach messages and key audiences where gaps have been identified.

The National Ocean Acidification Program Office can play a pivotal role in uniting key partners by promoting working relationships between other National Science and Technology Council Interagency Working Groups such as the Interagency Working Group on Aquaculture, U.S. agencies, NGOs, academia, and private businesses throughout the world at ongoing and developing venues. New partnerships may take the form of public-private partnerships, which have proven successful at uniting public, private, and philanthropic partners to address complex, cross-cutting issues.

International partnerships may form via new initiatives that address emerging cross-cutting issues while striving to promote sustainable development on bilateral, regional, and global levels. As previously mentioned, formal science and technology agreements can unite governments in research partnerships, which may serve education and outreach needs. Science and technology cooperation, in addition to grants for international cooperation, supports the establishment of science-based industries, encourages investment in national science infrastructure, education, and application of scientific standards, and it promotes international dialogue. Additionally, the National Ocean Acidification Program Office can form new international partnerships by leveraging existing relationships established through U.S. embassies, consulates, and missions. By building off of existing relationships, an international engagement strategy will have more relevant and achievable goals.

Goals

Education and outreach efforts are vital to fostering public understanding of environmental and socioeconomic impacts of ocean acidification and ensuring adequate stakeholder involvement in research and adaptation planning. Domestic and international engagement should supplement education and outreach efforts, as well as create partnerships that better enable goals from this and other themes to be achieved. The short-term goals represent recommended priorities if funding becomes available. The long-term goals also represent recommended priorities, but they may take longer to yield their full benefits and/or require completion of one or more short-term goals. Many of the following goals are already receiving some attention.

Short-term (3-5 years)

- Incorporate education and outreach functions directly into the National Ocean Acidification Program Office.
- Engage current Cooperative Extension and National and state Sea Grant offices to develop and implement outreach programs focused on ocean acidification.
- Launch a public web portal as an education and outreach interface of the National Ocean Acidification Program (complementary to data access portal described in Theme 7).
- Design an implementation strategy for education and outreach for ocean acidification which will:
    o Identify all domestic and international stakeholders in ocean acidification for education and outreach efforts;
    o Identify additional resources and partners required for education and outreach domestic and international efforts;
    o Link to existing partners, especially those that represent high-priority audiences.
    oIdentify potential new partnerships, especially with partners that represent high-priority audiences; and
    o Conduct a gap analysis to determine how the National Ocean Acidification Program Office will complement and progress ongoing education and outreach efforts.
- Solidify funding streams to foster development and maintenance of education, outreach, and engagement programs and activities.
- Facilitate ocean acidification data and information exchange among stakeholders (see Theme 7).
- Encourage and reward scientists doing ocean acidification research that are actively engaging the general public through seminars, web sites, and authorship of articles and books targeting a general audience.
- Provide incentives to researchers and laboratories supported by federal funds to engage in both formal and informal education efforts, and provide coordination of these efforts across the federal government.
- Establish a national mechanism that coordinates linkages between federally supported ocean acidification researchers and facilities and students, providing structured, meaningful, and sustained educational experiences, in the form of internships and fellowships.
- Evaluate the effectiveness of the National Ocean Acidification Program Office's education and outreach initiatives using short-term, measurable benchmarks.
- Make scientific assessments available to managers, policy makers, and the general public as useful education tools.

Long-term (10 years)

- Review and update the education and outreach strategic plan as new information is generated, the stakeholder and donor audiences change, partnerships are formed and evolve, education and outreach messages change, and as the effectiveness of ongoing education and outreach initiatives are determined.
- Create new partnerships, especially with partners that represent high-priority audiences.
- Evaluate the effectiveness the National Ocean Acidification Program Office's education and outreach initiatives using long-term measurable benchmarks.
- Support and offer a strong and complete suite of formal education opportunities and products.
- Serve as example of effective coordination across federal agencies for educational programs and initiatives.
- Be recognized by key stakeholders as providing useful, actionable, effective, and coordinated scientific information, guidance, and engagement.

Budget

The FY 2012 Budget allocated $807,000 to support education, outreach, and engagement efforts under the National Ocean Acidification Program (see Appendix 2 for more details). Agencies presently supporting ocean acidification education and outreach efforts include NASA, NOAA, NSF, and USGS.

Theme 7. Data Management and Integration

The success of the National Ocean Acidification enterprise will depend critically on effective data management and integration. Data must be shared and integrated across disciplinary boundaries, drawing marine biological data together with oceanographic data and providing intelligible information to social scientists, planners, educators, and the general public. Data must also be shared and integrated across organizational boundaries, blending data from diverse systems that were created to address distinct mission goals. Finally, data must be shared and integrated across data management technology boundaries that currently limit the interoperability between in situ observations and gridded fields such as satellite products, data synthesis products, and numerical model outputs.

The strategy for data management within the National Ocean Acidification Program must fit within a context of national data policies and existing programs. It must follow the guidelines of the National Ocean Policy (OPTF 2010), which includes a goal of "nationally consistent, derived data products" and "a robust information management system to allow easy access to and transparency of data and information necessary for planning."

Requirements and Recommendations

Strategic planning to meet the data management and integration needs of the National Ocean Acidification Program should build on lessons learned from successful data integration endeavors in related ocean research programs (Glover et al. 2006; NRC 2010a). Experience has shown that a data management system should be established early in the implementation of the program. We also know that, to be effective, the budget for data management should be about 10-20% of the total cost of the ocean acidification program, considering both hardware and competent staff. The OATF report to the ORRAP (2010) echoes these ideas asserting, "…there needs to be a permanent, national, interagency cyber-infrastructure system that ties together or stores in a few places, all relevant data archives relevant to ocean acidification." To help build and implement this vision, NOAA sponsored an interagency ocean acidification Data Management Workshop in March 2012. Representatives from across NOAA, from other ocean related science Federal agencies and from academia attended, representing expertise in data management and scientific research experience. Participants in the workshop recognized the need for a cooperative approach between scientists and data managers in order to achieve successful integration of the diverse ocean acidification data being collected. To that end, the emerging ocean acidification community represented at that workshop has developed a so-called Declaration of Interdependence, which articulates the goals and vision for ocean acidification data integration in the U.S with specific, actionable recommendations for interagency action (CIMOAD, 2012). An initial data management plan has also been drafted as a result of this workshop (NOAA, 2012).

Additional elements of the ocean acidification data management and integration strategy are: developing and maintaining a flexible and adaptable data access framework and web portal; ensuring timely availability of data, version control, and citations to data; defining and enforcing standards for sensor information management and metadata records; identifying a data archival center or centers to acquire, document, and provide authoritative access to ocean acidification data; and supporting data synthesis and modeling efforts.

Ocean Acidification Data Management Office

Early establishment of an Ocean Acidification Data Management Office under the National Program Office would be highly desirable in order to oversee the many complex connections between institutions and data systems that will be contributing to the Program (NRC 2010a; refer to Box 12 for examples). If ocean acidification data management functions must be embedded within an existing federally supported data management activity due to resource limitations, then it remains essential to employ staff members dedicated to a curatorship role for the ocean acidification data collection. To this end, the National Oceanographic Data Center has been designated to serve as the long-term archive for NOAA-funded ocean acidification data. Where possible, the National Oceanographic Data Center (NODC) will also serve the broader ocean acidification community through partnerships and leveraging of resources.

The model for integration, in order to respect the independence of data systems developed by the contributors, must be a system-of-systems outlook, such as has been articulated in numerous plans, including the U.S. Integrated Ocean Observing System Data Management and Communications (IOOS-DMAC) Plan (Hankin and the DMAC Steering Committee 2005), NOAA's Global Earth Observation-Integrated Data Environment (GEO-IDE) plan (U.S. Department of Commerce 2006), the European Union's SeaDataNet (Schaap 2009), the Global Earth Observation System of Systems (GEOSS) framework (Group on Earth Observations [GEO] 2005) and the emerging Federal data architecture being developed within the SOST ad hoc Biodiversity Working Group (Fornwall 2012). The Ocean Acidification Data Management Office must also manage a shared data analysis environment to support community data synthesis and integration activities and a framework for model intercomparison.

Box 12. Examples of key programs with data systems related to activities of the Ocean Acidification Data Management Office. Specific contributions of each effort to ocean acidification research will be addressed via the National Program Office and Implementation Plan.

NOAA:
- Integrated Ocean Observing System (IOOS 2009)
- Global Earth Observation-Integrated Data Environment (GEO-IDE) integration framework (U.S. Department of Commerce 2006)
- Pacific Marine Environmental Laboratory Ocean Carbon Program Data Portal
- National Oceanographic Data Center (NODC)

NSF-funded:
- Biological and Chemical Oceanography Data Management Office (BCO-DMO)
- Ocean Observatories Initiative CyberInfrastructure (OOI-CI)
- Earth Cube, an integrated data management infrastructure program

NASA:
- SeaBASS data base of in situ measurements related satellite fields
- Model outputs at the NASA Jet Propulsion Laboratory (JPL)

National Park Service (NPS):
- NPS Natural Resource Information Portal (NRInfo)

FWS:
- National Wildlife Refuge System (NWRS) Inventory and Monitoring Iniative Data Management System

EPA:
- Environmental Monitoring and Assessment Program (EMAP)

USGS:
- National Water Information System Water-quality Web Services3
- National Map
- Modeling Data Network
- Ocean Biogeographic Information System-USA

Department of Energy (DOE):
- Carbon Dioxide Information Analysis Center

Data Web Portal, Information Exchange, and Data Access Framework

As discussed in Theme 6, the FOARAM Act calls for the creation and maintenance of a Web portal for purposes of disseminating ocean acidification data and information across the spectrum of education, outreach, and research applications. Integrated ocean acidification information derived from the data need to help facilitate policymaking and education across disciplines, ideally by allowing interaction with these other data sets (e.g., pollution, nutrients). Users of ocean acidification data and scientists directly involved in the research efforts need to be able to locate, subset, download, and visualize relevant data and browse associated documentation and metadata. The National Ocean Acidification Program data management strategy must ensure that numerical data are made available through standards and protocols that are readily compatible with a broad range of desktop applications that perform statistical, numerical analysis, visualization, and geographic information system mapping and geospatial analysis. This will require close and ongoing consultation with user communities to determine the specific software tools that need to be supported. Creative procedures will need to be developed for extracting and sharing data once it is compiled. A metadata-driven, interoperable, services-based approach will enable the optimal integration of data sources. Capturing the uncertainties associated with the data will also be key for data integration and application to management decisions. There are existing entities within the Federal government that may address or include data relevant to ocean acidification; the proposed portal should work with these existing entities and leverage these efforts.

Timely Availability of Data

Meeting the management and research goals of the National Ocean Acidification Program will require open and timely access to data and information from both Federal agencies and non-federal partners. Cultural barriers often inhibit the timely and complete release of data and metadata more than technical data networking considerations (Riebesell et al. 2010). The National Ocean Acidification Program partners should strive continually towards a goal of releasing all data as rapidly as feasible and should work with its partners to remove data access barriers and minimize delays in making data available to users. Data availability guidelines for NOAA-funded ocean acidification data will comply with NOAA's procedural directives on data sharing (2 years; NOAA Environmental Data Management Committee, 2011).

Version Control and Citations to Data

In order to assure the quality of ocean acidification observations and assess problems with the ocean sensors that have been deployed, the ocean acidification monitoring program will include overlapping observations, such as ship tracks that periodically pass close to in situ mooring locations. The insights obtained through the analysis of differences between these observations will lead to re-processing of the raw observations – making adjustments for problems, such as drift in sensor calibrations where possible, and assigning quality-control flags to the resultant observations. This is but one illustration of the need for the data management system to track observations at multiple levels of processing. Reproducible access to the precise version of data cited in publications is vital both to the integrity of the scientific process and for understanding the appropriate usage of products derived from the data (Hankin et al. 2010). The Guide to Best Practices in Ocean Acidification Research and Data Reporting (Riebesell et al. 2010) provides useful guidance on the use of Digital Object Identifiers. The Ocean Acidification Data Management Office must apply due diligence to ensure that citations to data are reproducible, while recognizing this as an area of emerging technology with solutions that must evolve over time.

Sensor Information Management

The National Ocean Acidification Program calls for an aggressive program of research and development intended to advance the design of chemical and biological sensors. Implicit in this plan will be a parallel evolution in the protocols that must be followed in order to deploy and utilize the sensors effectively. The National Ocean Acidification Program data management strategy must therefore ensure that accurate and detailed information about the sensors, measurement protocols, and processing are reliably captured and made available with the data. It must retain and catalog this information together with the relevant measurements, so that future users of ocean acidification observations can assess the sources of uncertainty in the data. The National Ocean Acidification Program should strive for a successful model of managing both the observations and information about the observation procedures, utilizing a blend of computer technology and adherence to associated community protocols.

Metadata

Many of the data management goals articulated above rely upon proper handling of metadata (information about where, when, and how data were generated, and by whom). A vital responsibility of the Ocean Acidification Data Management Program will be to ensure that, to the degree feasible, metadata needs are addressed "before field programs begin" (Glover et al. 2006; NRC 2010a). Glover et al. (2006) indicated that metadata must go beyond "conventions for standard methods, names, and units, as well as an agreed-to list of metadata to be collected along with the data," to include detailed descriptions of sensors, platforms, and their histories. This knowledge lies with the scientists, engineers, and technicians who create, install, and manage sensors, perform analyses, and run models. Thus, the science plans for the ocean acidification observations, modeling, and synthesis programs have a key responsibility in data management; they must define and enforce the protocols needed to ensure that metadata are captured reliably and effectively. Metadata records generated by the National Ocean Acidification Program should be made available through appropriate standards to be discoverable by national and international data integration frameworks such as GEOSS and Geodata.gov. An interagency ocean acidification parameter group has been recently formed with members of the scientific and data management community to help coordinate the development and review of standardized ocean acidification vocabulary that resides in the Marine Metadata interoperability's website.

Archival

Ensuring the long-term preservation of the data assembled under the National Ocean Acidification Program will be a responsibility of the Ocean Acidification Data Management Office. The NRC report (2010a) suggests a sensible strategy: "The Program should identify appropriate data center(s) for archiving of ocean acidification data or, if existing data centers are inadequate, the Program should create its own." The National Oceanographic Data Center at NOAA preserves originator data as submitted by the provider. NODC also has a data access infrastructure that allows for data visualization and data sub-setting, as well as access to highly quality controlled, authoritative data sets.

A number of agencies have been exploring archival services for model outputs, but to date, there is no established and funded program of this sort to handle ocean model outputs. Furthermore, instituting the archival of a new model output data stream will typically incur non-trivial costs, the data volumes are usually considerable and increase over time, and the process of implementing responsible archival procedures involves careful creation and maintenance of metadata that captures the configuration of the model code and the specification of initial and boundary conditions. Standards and procedures to capture ocean acidification-related metadata do not yet exist, so this presents an additional development cost. However, rapid strides are being made in the development of metadata standards through model output management efforts such as the WCRP's Coupled Model Intercomparison Project, Phase 5 (CMIP5), which operates out of the Program for Climate Model Diagnosis and Intercomparison.

Support for Social Science Data, Data Synthesis, and Modeling

Theme 5 addresses the need for socioeconomic data to help the nation develop informed responses to ocean acidification. Similar archival and data management procedures need to be implemented for this growing area of research. The NSF Directorate of Geosciences has embarked on a program, Earth Cube, which seeks to develop a transformative approach to integrating earth systems data across the domains of natural and social sciences. Coastal SEES, an element of the cross-foundation SEES, will specifically require the integration of social science data with environmental data. It is expected that the interagency ocean acidification research program will be able to build on these NSF-supported activities. In Theme 1 of this strategic plan, we discuss the importance of data synthesis as a component of ocean acidification research. Effective data management is required to support such an activity in a collaborative, multi-agency context. A successful model of such a system is found in the international Surface Ocean Carbon Atlas (SOCAT), project, a synthesis activity under the auspices of the International Ocean Carbon Coordination Project. The Ocean Acidification Data Management Office should strive to create a community "electronic commons" analogous to what SOCAT has provided. The electronic commons should be an environment in which scientists can evaluate data quality across the entire ocean acidification data collection, annotate the data with relevant insights, generate interpolated fields, and investigate outliers from these interpolated fields. As experience in the WCRP Coupled Model Intercomparison Projects (e.g., WCRP/CMIP3) has demonstrated, ocean acidification model intercomparison projects will also succeed at a much higher level if due consideration is given to data management support, including capturing and serving detailed model metadata (Williams et al. 2009).

Goals

A significant effort will be required to integrate different types of ocean acidification data sets (physical, chemical, biological, geological, and societal) from several agencies. A dedicated data management team will be required to perform this data integration. Some of the data management goals listed below are already receiving some attention, but a coordinated ocean acidification data management effort has yet to be initiated. The short-term goals represent recommended priorities if funding becomes available. The long-term goals also represent recommended priorities, but they may take longer to yield their full benefits and/or require completion of one or more short-term goals.

Short-term (3-5 years)
* Establish an Ocean Acidification Data Management Program (or Office) or a leadership project embedded within an existing Federally-supported data management activity with staff members dedicated to a curatorship role for the ocean acidification data collection. Under the guidance of this program or project:
    o Develop an initial data access web portal (complementary to education and outreach portal described in Theme 6).
    o Negotiate and implement system-specific approaches to interagency interoperability.
    o Develop a catalog of relevant data and documentation.
    o To the degree feasible, make data and metadata accessible through uniform standards and protocols.
    o Establish tools and procedures to support community-wide data synthesis, including careful control over versions of data.
    o Establish initial collaborative relationships (domestic and international) and procedures to ensure archival of the data.
    o Establish timeliness and data quality policies in conjunction with the science community.
    o Harmonize with the emerging IOOS framework.
    o The sub-disciplines of ocean acidification should self-organize around common procedures for collecting and documenting ocean acidification data.

Long-term (10 year)
* Determine the components of the ocean acidification data access framework.
* Develop true system-of-systems integrated data and metadata exchange.
* Automate collection of metadata from "smart" sensors where feasible.

Budget
Several agencies have data management programs that could support the goals of this theme. The FY 2012 Budget allocated $440,000 to support data management and integration (see Appendix 2 for more details). Agencies presently supporting ocean acidification data management and integration efforts include NOAA, NSF, and USGS.

References

Andersson A, Gledhill D. 2013. Ocean Acidification and Coral Reefs: Effects on Breakdown, Dissolution, and Net Ecosystem Calcification. J Annual Review of Marine Science 5(1): 321-348.

Andersson AJ, Kuffner IB, Mackenzie FT, Jokiel PL, Rodgers KS, Tan A. 2009. Net loss of CaCO3 from a subtropical calcifying community due to seawater acidification: mesocosm-scale experimental evidence. Biogeosciences 6:1811–23

Archer D, Kheshgi H, Maier-Reimer E (1998) Dynamics of fossil fuel CO2 neutralization by marine CaCO3. Global Biogeochem Cycles 12:259–276

Balch WM, Drapeau DT, Bowler BC, Booth E. 2007. Prediction of pelagic calcification rates using satellite measurements. Deep-Sea Research, Part II 54:478–495.

Barton A, Hales B, Waldbusser GG, Langdon C, Feely RA. 2012. The Pacific oyster, Crassotrea gigas, shows negative correlation to naturally elevated carbon dioxide levels: Implications for near-term ocean acidification effects. Limnology and Oceanography, 57:698-710.

Borges AV, Alin SR, Chavez FP, Vlahos P, Johnson KS, Holt JT, Balch WM, Bates N, Brainard R, Cai W-J, Chen CTA, Currie K, Dai M, Degrandpre M, Delille B, Dickson A, Evans W, Feely RA, Friederich GE, Gong G-C, Hales B, Hardman-Mountford N, Hendee J, Hernandez-Ayon JM, Hood M, Huertas E, Hydes D, Ianson D, Krasakopoulou E, Litt E, Luchetta A, Mathis J, McGillis WR, Murat A, Newton J, Ólafsson J, Omar A, Perez FF, Sabine C, Salisbury JE, Salm R, Sarma VVSS, Schneider B, Sigler M, Thomas H, Turk D, Vandemark D, Wanninkhof R, Ward B. 2010. A global sea surface carbon observing system: Inorganic and organic carbon dynamics in coastal oceans. In: Hall J, Harrison DE, Stammer D (eds). Proceedings of OceanObs'09: Sustained Ocean Observations and Information for Society, 21-25 September 2009, Venice, Italy, ESA Publication WPP-306.

Brainard R, Moffitt R, Timmers M, Paulay G, Plaisance L, Knowlton N, Caley J, Fohrer F, Charette A, Meyer C, Toonen R, Godwin S, Martin J, Harris L, Geller J, Moews M. 2009. Autonomous Reef Monitoring Structures (ARMS): A tool for monitoring indices of biodiversity in the Pacific Islands. 11th Pacific Science Inter-Congress, Papeete, Tahiti (http://intellagence.eu.com/psi2009/output_directory/cd1/Data/articles/000442.pdf).

Brander LM, Rehdanz K, Tol RSJ, Beukering PJH. 2009. The economic impact of ocean acidification on coral reefs. ESRI Working Paper 282, Economic and Social Research Institute (http://www.tara.tcd.ie/handle/2262/27779).

Briffa M, de la Hayea K, Munday PL. 2012. High CO2 and marine animal behaviour: Potential mechanisms and ecological consequences. Marine Pollution Bulletin 64:1519–1528.

Buddemeier RW, Kinzie RA. 1976. Coral growth. Oceanography and Marine Biology: An Annual Review 14:183-225.

Cai WJ, Hu X, Huang WJ, Murrell MC, Lehrter JC, Lohrenz SE, Chou WC, Zhai W, Hollibaugh, JT, Wang Y, Zhao P, Guo X, Gundersen K, Dai M, & Gong GC. 2011. Acidification of subsurface coastal waters enhanced by eutrophication. Nature Geoscience, 4(11), 766-770.

Caldeira K, Wickett ME. 2003. Oceanography: Anthropogenic carbon and ocean pH. Nature 425:365. Caldeira K, Wickett ME. 2005. Ocean model predictions of chemistry changes from carbon dioxide emissions to the atmosphere and ocean. Journal of Geophysical Research 110, C09S04 (doi:10.1029/2004JC002671).

Caswell, H. 2001. Matrix population models. Sinauer Associates. Sunderaland, MA. USA. Chalker BE, Barnes DJ. 1990. Gamma densitometry for the measurement of skeletal density. Coral Reefs 9:11-23.

Consortium for the Integrated Management of Ocean Acidification Data (CIMOAD). 2012. Declaration of Interdependence of Ocean Acidification Data Management Activities in the U.S. OA Data Management Workshop, 2012, Seattle, WA. http://www.nodc.noaa.gov/media/pdf/oceanacidification/Declaration_May312012.pdf

Cooley SR, Doney SC. 2009. Anticipating ocean acidification's economic consequences for commercial fisheries. Environmental Research Letters 4, 024007 (stacks.iop.org/ERL/4/024007).

Costello, CJ, Adams, RM, and Polasky, S. 1998. The value of El Nino forecasts in the management of salmon: a stochastic dynamic assessment. American Journal of Agricultural Economics, Vol. 80. No. 4, pp.   765-777.

Dickson AG, Sabine CL, Christian JR (eds). 2007. Guide to Best Practices for Ocean CO2 Measurements. PICES Special Publication 3, IOCCP Report No. 8, North Pacific Marine Science Organization.

Doney SC, Fabry VJ, Feely RA, Kleypas JA. 2009. Ocean acidification: The other CO2 problem. Annual Re view of Marine Science 1:169–192.

Doney SC, Mahowald N, Lima I, Feely RA, Mackenzie FT, Lamarque JF, Rasch PJ. 2007 Impact of anthropogenic atmospheric nitrogen and sulfur deposition on ocean acidification and the inorganic carbon system, Proc. Natl. Acad. Sci 104:14580–14585

Dore JE, Lukas R, Sadler DW, Church MJ, Karl DM. 2009. Physical and biogeochemical modulation of ocean acidification in the central North Pacific. Proceedings of the National Academy of Sciences 106(30):12235–12240.

Easterling WE, III, Hurd BH, Smith JB. 2004. Coping with global climate change: The role of adaptation in the United States. Prepared for the Pew Center on Global Climate Change (http://www.pewclimate. org/docUploads/Adaptation.pdf).

Evans TG, Hofmann GE. 2012. Defining the limits of physiological plasticity in marine organisms: how gene expression profiling can aid in predicting the consequences of ocean change. Phil. Trans. Of Royal Society B 267:1733-1745.

Fabricius, KE, Langdon C, Uthicke S, Humphrey C, Noonan S, De'ath G, Okazaki R, Muehllehner N, Glas MS, Lough JM. 2011. Losers and winners in coral reefs acclimatized to elevated carbon dioxide concentrations. Nature Climate Change 1(3): 165-169.

Fabry VJ, Langdon C, Balch WM, Dickson AG, Feely RA, Hales B, Hutchins DA, Kleypas JA, Sabine CL. 2008. Present and Future Impacts of Ocean Acidification on Marine Ecosystems and Biogeochemical Cycles, Report of the Ocean Carbon and Biogeochemistry Scoping Workshop on Ocean Acidification Research, 9-11 October 2007, La Jolla, CA.

Fabry VJ, Seibel BA, Feely RA, Orr JC. 2008. Impacts of ocean acidification on marine fauna and ecosystem processes. ICES Journal of Marine Science, 65: 414–432.

Feely RA, Sabine CL, Lee K, Berelson W, Kleypas J, Fabry VJ, Millero FJ. 2004. Impact of anthropogenic CO2 on the CaCO3 system in the oceans. Science 305:362–366.

Feely RA, Doney SC, Cooley SR (2009) Present conditions and future changes in a high CO2 world. Oceanography 22:36-47.

Feely RA, Fabry VJ, Dickson A, Gattuso JP, Bijma J, Riebesell U, Doney S, Turley C, Saino T, Lee K, Anthony K, Kleypas J. 2010. An international observational network for ocean acidification. In Hall J, Harrison DE, Stammer D (eds). Proceedings of OceanObs'09: Sustained Ocean Observations and Information for Society, 21-25 September 2009, Venice, Italy, ESA Publication WPP-306.

Feely RA, Klinger T, Newton JA, Chadsey M. 2012. Scientific Summary of Ocean Acidification in Washington State Marine Waters. NOAA OAR Special Report. [In preparation].

Findlay HS, Wood HL, Kendall MA, Spicer JI, R. Twitchett J, Widdicombe S. 2009. Calcification, a physiological process to be considered in the context of the whole organism. Biogeo sciences Discussion 6: 2267–2284.

Follows MJ, Dutkiewicz S, Grant S, Chisholm S. 2007. Emergent biogeography of microbial communities in a model ocean. Science 315:1843–1846.

Form AU, Riebesell U. 2012. Acclimation to ocean acidification during long-term CO2 exposure in the cold water coral *Lophelia pertusa*. Global Change Biology 18(3):843-853.

Fornwall, M.F., Gisiner B., Simmons S.E., Moustafid H., Canonico G., Halpin P., Goldstein P., Fitch R., Weise M., Cyr N., Palka D., Collins D. 2012. Expanding Biological Data Standards Development Processes for US IOOS: Visual Line Transect Observing Community for Mammal, Bird, and Turtle Data. http://www.iooc.us/summit/white-paper-guidelines/community-white-paper-submissions/

Garrard SL, Hunter RC, Frommerl AY, Lane AC, Phillips JC, Cooper R, Dineshram R, Cardini U, McCoy SJ, Arnberg M, Rodrigues Alves BG, Annane S, de Orte MR, Kumar A, Aguirre- Martinez GV, Maneja RH, Basallote MD, Ape F, Torstensson A, Bjoerk MM. 2012. Biological impacts of ocean acidification: a postgraduate perspective on research priorities. Marine Biology doi: 10.1007/s00227-012-2033-3

Gattuso JP, Frankignoulle M, Bourge I, Romaine S, Buddemeier RW. 1998. Effect of calcium carbonate saturation of seawater on coral calcification. Global and Planetary Change 18:37–46.

Gattuso JP, Hansson L. 2011. Ocean acidification, Oxford University Press, 1–20.

Gilman SE, Urban MC, Tewksbury J, Gilchrist GW, Holt RD. 2010. A framework for community interactions under climate change. Trends in Ecology & Evolution 25:325–331.

Gledhill DK, Wanninkhof R, Millero FJ, Eakin M. 2008. Ocean acidification of the greater Caribbean region, 1996-2006. Journal of Geophysical Research, 113, C10031 .

Glover DM, Chandler CL, Doney SC, Buesseler KO, Heimerdinger G, Bishop JKB, Flierl GR. 2006. The U.S. JGOFS Data Management Experience. Deep Sea Research Part II: Topical Studies in Oceanography 53:793-802.

Group on Earth Observations (GEO). 2005. The Global Earth Observation System of Systems (GEOSS) 10-Year Implementation Plan (http://www.earthobservations.org/documents/10-Year%20Implementation%20Plan.pdf).

Guinotte, JM, Fabry VJ. 2008. Ocean acidification and its potential effects on marine ecosystems. Annals of the New York Academy of Sciences 1134:320-342.

Hall J, Harrison DE, Stammer D (eds). 2010. Proceedings of OceanObs'09: Sustained Ocean Observations and Information for Society, 21-25 September 2009, Venice, Italy, ESA Publication WPP-306.

Hankin S. and the Data Management and Communications Steering Committee. 2005. Data Management and Communications Plan for Research and Operational Integrated Ocean Observing Systems: I. Interoperable Data Discovery, Access, and Archive, The National Office for Integrated and Sustained Ocean Observations Ocean.US Publication No. 6, Arlington, VA (http://www.ioos.gov/library/dmac_plan_2005.pdf).

Hankin S, Bermudez L, Blower JD, Blumenthal B, Casey KS, Fornwall M, Graybeal J, Guralnick RP, Habermann T, Howlett E, Keeley B, Mendelssohn R, Schlitzer R, Signell R, Snowden D, Woolf A. 2010. Data management for the ocean sciences – Perspectives for the next decade. In: Hall J, Harrison DE, Stammer D (eds). Proceedings of OceanObs'09: Sustained Ocean Observations and Information for Society, 21-25 September 2009, Venice, Italy, ESA Publication WPP-306.

Havenhand JN, Schlegel P. 2009. Near-future levels of ocean acidification do not affect sperm motility and fertilization kinetics in the oyster *Crassostrea gigas*. Biogeosciences, 6:3009-3015.

Hoegh-Guldberg O, Mumby PJ, Hooten AJ, Steneck RS, Greenfield P, Gomez E, Harvell CD, Sale PF, Edwards AJ, Caldeira K, Knowlton N, Eakin CM, Iglesias-Prieto R, Muthiga N, Bradbury RH, Dubi A, Hatziolos ME. 2007. Coral reefs under rapid climate change and ocean acidification. Science 318:1737.

Hoffmann LJ, Breitbarth E, Boyd PW, Hunter KA. 2012. Influence of ocean warming and acidification on trace metal biogeochemistry. Marine Ecology Progress Series 470:191-205.

Holcomb M, McCorkle DC, Cohen AL. 2010. Long-term effects of nutrient and CO_2 enrichment on the temperate coral Astrangia poculata. Journal of Experimental Marine Biology and Ecology 386:27-33.

Hönisch B, Hemming NG, Archer D, Siddall M, McManus JF. 2009. Atmospheric carbon dioxide concentration across the Mid-Pleistocene Transition. Science 324:1551–1554.

Hönisch B, Ridgwell A, Schmidt DN, Thomas E, Gibbs SJ, Sluijs A, Zeebe R, Kump L, Martindale RC, Greene SE, Kiessling W, Ries J, Zachos JC, Royer DL, Barker S, Marchitto Jr. TM, Moyer R, Pelejero C, Ziveri P, Foster GL, Williams B. 2012. The geological record of ocean acidification. Science 335:1058–1063.

Hope C. 2006. The marginal impact of CO_2 from PAGE2002: An integrated assessment model incorporating the IPCC's five reasons for concern. Integrated Assessment Journal 6:19–56.

Huesemann MH, Skillman AD, Crecelius EA. 2002. The inhibition of marine nitrification by ocean disposal of carbon dioxide. Marine Pollution Bulletin 44:142–148.

Hurlbert, SH, 1984, Pseudoreplication and the Design of Ecological Field Experiments, Ecological Monographs, 54(2): 187-211.

Hutchins DA, Mulholland MR, Fu FX. 2009. Nutrient cycles and marine microbes in a CO_2-enriched ocean. Oceanography 22:128–45.

Iglesias-Rodriguez MD, Halloran PR, Rickaby RE, Hall IR, Colmenero-Hidalgo E, Gittins JR, Green DR, Tyrrell T, Gibbs SJ, von Dassow P, Rehm E, Armbrust EV, Boessenkool KP. 2008. Phytoplankton calcification in a high-CO_2 world. Science 320:336.

Integrated Ocean Observing System (IOOS). 2009. Data Management and Communications Concept of Operations, Version 1.5, National Oceanic and Atmospheric Administration (http://www.ioos.gov/library/dmac_cops_v1_5_01_09_09.pdf).

Intergovernmental Panel on Climate Change (IPCC). 2013. Climate Change 2013: The Physical Science Basis. Contribution of Working Group I to the Fifth Assessment Report of the Intergovernmental Panel on Climate Change [Stocker, T.F., D. Qin, G.-K. Plattner, M. Tignor, S.K. Allen, J. Boschung, A. Nauels, Y. Xia, V. Bex and P.M. Midgley (eds.)]. Cambridge University Press, Cambridge, United Kingdom and New York, NY, USA, pp. 1535.

Intergovernmental Panel on Climate Change (IPCC), 2011. Workshop Report of the Intergovernmental Panel on Climate Change Workshop on Impacts of Ocean Acidification on Marine Biology and Eco systems. IPCC Working Group II Technical Support Unit, Carnegie Institution, Stanford, California, USA, pp. 164.

Jackson LE, Kurtz JC, Fisher WS (eds). 2000. Evaluation Guidelines for Ecological Indicators. U.S. Environmental Protection Agency, Office of Research and Development, Research Triangle Park, NC. EPA/620/R-99/005.

Johnson MD, Carpenter RC. 2012. Ocean acidification and warming decrease calcification in the crustose coralline alga Hydrolithon onkodes and increases susceptibility to grazing. Journal of Experimental Marine Biology and Ecology 434/435:94-101.

Joint I, Doney SC and Karl DM. 2010. Will ocean acidification affect marine microbes? The International Society for Microbial Ecology Journal, published online (doi:10.1038/ismej.2010.79).

Juranek, LW, Feely RA, Peterson WT, Alin SR, Hales B, Lee K, Sabine CL, Peterson J. 2009. A novel method for determination of aragonite saturation state on the continental shelf of central Oregon using multi-parameter relationships with hydrographic data. Geophysical Research Letters 36, L24601 (doi:10.1029/2009GL040778).

Kleypas JA, Buddemeier RW, Archer D, Gattuso J-P, Langdon C, Opdyke BN. 1999. Geochemical consequences of increased atmospheric carbon dioxide on coral reefs. Science 284: 118–120.

Kleypas JA, Langdon C. 2006. Coral Reefs and Changing Seawater Carbonate Chemistry. In Phinney J, Hoegh-Guldberg O, Kleypas J, Skirving W, Strong A (eds.). Coastal and Estuarine Studies 61 – Coral Reefs and Climate Change: Science and Management, American Geophysical Union, Washington, DC, pp. 73–110.

Kleypas JA, Feely RA, Fabry VJ, Langdon C, Sabine CL, Robbins LL. 2006. Impacts of Ocean Acidification on Coral Reefs and Other Marine Calcifiers: A Guide to Future Research. Report of a workshop held 18–20 April 2005, St. Petersburg, FL, sponsored by NSF, NOAA, and the U.S. Geological Survey.

Kroeker KJ, Kordas RL, Crim RN, Singh GG. 2010a. Meta-analysis reveals negative yet variable effects of ocean acidifcation on marine organisms. Ecology Letters 13:1419-1434.

Kroeker KJ, Micheli F, Gambi MC, Martz TR. 2011b. Divergent ecosystem responses within a benthic marine community to ocean acidification. Proceedings of the National Academy of Sciences of the United States of America 108:14515-14520.

Kroeker KJ, Kordas RL, Crim R, Hendricks IE, Ramajo L, Singh GS, Duarte CM, Gattuso JP. 2013. Impacts of ocean acidification on marine organisms: quantifying sensitivities and interaction with warming. doi:10.1111/gcb.12179

Kump, L.R., T.J. Bralower, and A. Ridgwell. 2009. Ocean acidification in deep time. Oceanography 22:94–107.

Kurihara H. 2008. Effects of CO_2-driven ocean acidification on the early developmental stages of invertebrates. Mar. Ecol. Prog. Ser 373:275–284.

Lammers MO, Brainard RE, Au WWL, Mooney TA, Wong KB. 2008. An ecological acoustic recorder (EAR) for long-term monitoring of biological and anthropogenic sounds on coral reefs and other marine habitats. Journal of the Acoustical Society of America 123:1720–1728.

Lohbeck KT, Riebesell U, Reusch TBH. 2012. Adaptive evolution of a key phytoplankton species to ocean acidification. Nature Geoscience 5:346-351.

Lüthi D, Le Floch M, Bereiter B, Blunier T, Barnola J-M, Siegenthaler U, Raynaud D, Jouzel J, Fischer H, Kawamura K, Stocker TF. 2008 High-resolution carbon dioxide concentration record 650,000-800,000 years before present. Nature 453:379–382.

Mathis, J.T.,Byrne, R.H., McNeil, C.L., Pickart, R.P., Juranek, L., Liu, S., Ma, J., Easley, R.A.,

Elliot, M.W., Cross, J.N., Reisdorph, S. C., Morison, J., Lichendorph, T., Feely, R.A., 2012. Storm Induced Upwelling of High pCO2 Waters onto the Continental Shelf of the Western Arctic Ocean and Implications for Carbonate Mineral Saturation States. Geophys.Res. Lett. Vol. 39, L07606

Melzner F, Stange P, Trübenbach K, Thomsen J, Casties I, Panknin U. Gorb SN, Gutowska MA. 2011. Food supply and seawater pCO2 impact calcification and internal shell dissolution in the blue mussel Mytilus edulis. PLoS ONE 6:e24223.

Metz B, Davidson OR, Bosch PR, Dave R, Meyer LA (eds). 2007. Climate Change 2007: Mitigation of Climate Change. Contribution of Working Group III to the Fourth Assessment Report of the Inter governmental Panel on Climate Change, Cambridge University Press, Cambridge, UK.

Millero FJ, Woosley R, DiTrolio B, Waters J. 2009. Effect of ocean acidification on the speciation of metals in seawater. Oceanography 22:72–85.

Moore, C. 2011. Welfare impacts of ocean acidification: an integrated assessment model of the US mollusk fishery. U.S. EPA, National Center for Environmental Economics, Working Paper #11-06.

Narita, D., Redhanz, K. and Tol, RSJ. 2012. Economic costs of ocean acidification: a look into the impacts on global fish production. Climate Change, 113:1049-1063.

National Oceanic and Atmospheric Administration (NOAA). 2010b. A Climate Service in NOAA: Draft Vision and Strategic Framework, Version 8.1 (http://www.noaa.gov/climateresourc es/resources/NCS_Vision_and_Strategic_Framework_Draft.pdf).

Nilsson GE, Dixson DL, Domenici P, McCormick MI, Sørensen C, Watson S, Munday PL. 2012. Near-future carbon dioxide levels alter fish behaviour by interfering with neurotransmitter function. Nature Climate change 2:201- 204.

NOAA Environmental Data Management Committee. 2011. NOAA Data Sharing Policy for Grants and Cooperative Agreements Procedural Directive Version 2.0. https://www.nosc.noaa.gov/EDMC/ documents/EDMC-PD-DSP.pdf

NOAA Ocean Acidification Steering Committee. 2010. NOAA Ocean and Great Lakes Acidification Re search Plan, NOAA Special Report, 143 pp.

NOAA Ocean Acidification Data Management Team. 2012. Interagency Ocean Acidification Data Management Plan: Draft One. OA Data Management Workshop, 2012, Seattle, WA. http://www. nodc.noaa.gov/media/pdf/oceanacidification/InteragencyOADataMgmtPlan_June2012-2.pdf.

National Research Council (NRC). 2010a. Ocean Acidification: A National Strategy to Meet the Challenges of a Changing Ocean. Committee on the Development of an Integrated Strategy for Ocean Acidification Monitoring, Research and Impacts Assessment, National Academies Press, Washington, DC.

National Research Council (NRC). 2010b. Informing an Effective Response to Climate Change. The National Academies Press. Washington, DC.

Nilsson GE, Dixson DL, Domenici P, McCormick MI, Sorensen C, Watson S-A, Munday PL. 2012. Near-future carbon dioxide levels alter fish behavior by interfering with neurotransmitter function. Nature Climate Change 2:201-204.

Nordhaus W. 2008. A question of balance: Weighing the options on global warming policies. Yale University Press, New Haven, CT.

Ocean Policy Task Force (OPTF). 2010. Final Recommendations of the Interagency Ocean Policy Task Force. The White House Council on Environmental Quality, Washington, DC (http://www. whitehouse.gov/files/documents/OPTF_FinalRecs.pdf).

Ocean Research and Resources Advisory Panel (ORRAP) 2010. Ocean Acidification Task Force, Summary of Work Completed and Draft Recommendations. Presentation to ORRAP, 27 July 2010. Alaska SeaLife Center, Seward, AK.

Orr JC, Fabry VF, Aumont O, Bopp L, Doney SC, Feely RA, Gnanadesikan A, Gruber N, Ishida A, Joos F, Key RM, Lindsay K, Maier-Reimer E, Matear R, Monfray P, Mouchet A, Najjar RG, Plattner G-K, Rodgers K-B, Sabine CL, Sarmiento JL, Schlitzer R, Slater RD, Totterdell IJ, Weirig M-F, Yamanaka Y, Yool A. 2005. Anthropogenic ocean acidification over the twenty-first century and its impact on calcifying organisms. Nature 437:681–686.

Orr JC, Caldeira K, Fabry V, Gattuso J-P, Haugan P, Lehodey P, Pantoja S, Pörtner H-O, Riebesell U, Trull T, Hood M, Urban E, Broadgate W. 2009. Research Priorities for Ocean Acidification, report from the Second Symposium on the Ocean in a High-CO2 World, Monaco, October 6-9, 2008, convened by SCOR, UNESCO-IOC, IAEA, and IG (http://ioc3.unesco.org/oanet/HighCO2World.html).

Oschlies A, Blackford J, Doney SC, Gehlen M. 2010. Modeling considerations. In Riebesell U, Fabry VJ, Hansson L, Gattuso J-P (eds.). 2010. Guide to Best Practices for Ocean Acidification Research and Data Reporting. Publications Office of the European Union, Luxembourg, 233–242.

Pansch C, Nasrolahi A, Appelhans YS, Wahl M. 2012. Impacts of ocean warming and acidification on the larval development of the barnacle *Amphibalanus improvisus*. Journal of Experimental Marine Biology and Ecology 420-421: 48-55

Pelejero C, Calvo E, Hoegh-Guldberg O. 2010. Paleo-perspectives on ocean acidification. Trends in Ecology & Evolution 25:332–344.

Pörtner H-O. 2008. Ecosystem effects of ocean acidification in times of ocean warming: A physiologist's view. Marine Ecology Progress Series 373:203–217.

Pörtner, H.O., et al. 2011: Nekton. In: Ocean Acidification [Gattuso, J.P., and L. Hansson (eds.)]. Oxford University Press.

Raven J, Caldeira K, Elderfield H, Hoegh-Guldberg O, Liss P, Riebesell U, Shepherd J, Turley C, Watson A. 2005. Ocean Acidification Due to Increasing Atmospheric Carbon Dioxide. Royal Society, London, UK.

Ridgwell A, Zeebe, RE. 2005. The role of the global carbonate cycle in the regulation and evolution of the Earth system. Earth and Planetary Science Letters 234(3): 299-315.

Ridgwell A, Schmidt, DN. 2010. Past constraints on the vulnerability of marine calcifiers to massive carbon dioxide release. Nature Geoscience 3(3): 196-200.

Riebesell U, Fabry VJ, Hansson L, Gattuso JP (eds.). 2010. Guide to Best Practices for Ocean Acidification Research and Data Reporting. Publications Office of the European Union, Luxembourg.

Ries, JB, Cohen AL, McCorkle DC. 2009. Marine calcifiers exhibit mixed responses to CO2-induced ocean acidification. Geology 37:1057–1152.

Robbins LL, Yates K, Feely R, Fabry V. 2010. Monitoring and Assessment of Ocean Acidification in the Arctic Ocean: A Scoping Paper, Open-File Report 2010–1227, U.S. Geological Survey, Reston, VA (http://pubs.usgs.gov/of/2010/1227/).

Sabine CL, Feely RA, Gruber N, Key RM, Lee K, Bullister JL, Wanninkhof R, Wong CS, Wallace DWR, Tilbrook B, Millero FJ, Peng TH, Kozyr A, Ono T, Rios AF. 2004. The oceanic sink for anthropogenic CO2. Science 305:367–371.

Schaap DMA. 2009. Development of Marine Data Management Infrastructures in Europe (SeaDataNet), Presented at: Twentieth Session of the IOC Committee on International Oceanographic Data and Information Exchange. (http://www.oceandocs.org/bit stream/1834/2977/1/IOC_IODE_XX_23_SeaDataNet.pdf).

Semiletov IP, Pipko II, Repina I, Shakhova NE. 2007. Carbonate chemistry dynamics and carbon dioxide fluxes across the atmosphere-ice-water interface in the Arctic Ocean. Journal of Marine Systems 66:204–226.

Silverman J, Lazar B, Cao L, Caldiera K, Erez J. 2009. Coral reefs may start dissolving when atmospheric CO2 doubles. Geophys. Res. Lett. 36:L05606

Silverman J, Lazar B, Erez J. 2007. Effect of aragonite saturation, temperature, and nutrients on the community calcification rate of a coral reef. Journal of Geophysical Research, 112, C05004 .

Simpson SD, Munday P, Wittenrich M, Manassa R, Dixson D, Gagliano M, Yan H. 2011. Ocean acidification erodes crucial auditory behaviour in a marine fish. Biology Letters 7:917–920.

Stearns, S.C. 1992. The evolution of life histories. Oxford University Press, New York, NY. USA.

Steinacher M, Joos F, Frolicher TL, Plattner GK, Doney SC. 2009. Imminent ocean acidification in the Arctic projected with the NCAR global coupled carbon cycle-climate model. Biogeosciences. 6:515–533.

Sunda WG, Cai WJ. 2012. Eutrophication Induced CO2-Acidification of Subsurface Coastal Waters: Interactive Effects of Temperature, Salinity, and Atmospheric PCO2. Environmental Science & Technology. 46:10651–10659.

Sunday JM, Crim RN, Harley CDG, Hart MW. 2011. Quantifying rates of evolutionary adaptation in response to ocean acidification. PLoS One 6:e22881.

Sueur J, Aubin T, Simonis C. 2008. Seewave, a free modular tool for sound analysis and synthesis. Bioacoustics 18:213–226.

Suzuki A, Kawahata H. 2003. Carbon budget of coral reef systems: an overview of observations in fringing reefs, barrier reefs and atolls in the Indo-pacific region. Tellus, 55B: 428–444.

Talmage SC, Gobler CJ. 2010. Effects of past, present, and future ocean carbon dioxide concentrations on the growth and survival of larval shellfish. Proceedings of the National Academy of Sciences of the United States of America 107:17246-17251.

Tol R. 2002. Estimates of the damage costs of climate change. Part 1: Benchmark estimates. Environmental and Resource Economics 21:47–73

Tribollet A, Godinot C, Atkinson M, Langdon C. 2009. Effects of elevated pCO2 on dissolution of coral carbonates by microbial euendoliths. Glob. Biogeochem. Cycles 23:GB3008

U.S. Department of Commerce, NOAA, Data Management Committee (DMC) Data Management Integration Team (DMIT) 2006. NOAA Global Earth Observation Integrated Data Environment (GEO-IDE) Concept of Operations Version 3.3 (www.nosc.noaa.gov/docs/products/NOAA_GEO-IDE_CONOPS-v3-3.doc).

Waldbusser GG, Voigt EP, Bergschneider H, Green MA, Newell RIE. 2011. Biocalcification in the Easter oyster (Crassotrea virginica) in relation to long-term trends in Chesapeake Bay pH. Estuaries Coasts 34:221-231.

Walther, Kathleen; Anger, Klaus; Pörtner, Hans-Otto (2010): Impact of ocean acidification and warming on the larval development of the spider crab *Hyas araneus* from different latitudes (54° vs 79°N). Marine Ecology-Progress Series, 417, 159-170

Williams D, Ananthakrishnan R, Bernholdt D, Bharathi S, Brown D, Chen M, Chervenak A, Cinquini L, Drach R, Foster I, Fox P, Fraser P, Garcia J, Hankin S, Jones P, Middleton D, Schwidder J, Schweitzer R, Schuler R, Shoshani A, Siebenlist F, Sim A, Strand W, Su M, Wilhelmi N. 2009. The Earth Systems Grid, Enabling Access to Multimodel Climate Simulation Data. Bulletin of the American Meteorological Society 90:195–205.

Yates KK, Halley RB. 2003. Measuring coral reef community metabolism using new benthic chamber technology. Coral Reefs 22:247–255.

Yates KK, Halley RB. 2006a. CO32- concentration and pCO2 thresholds for calcification and dissolution on the Molokai reef flat, Hawaii. Biogeosciences 3:1–13.

Yates KK, Halley RB. 2006b. Diurnal variation in rates of calcification and carbonate sediment dissolution in Florida Bay. Estuaries and Coasts 29:24–39.

Zachos JC, Rohl U, Schellenberg SA, Sluijs A, Hodell DA, Kelly DC, Thomas E, Nicolo M, Raffi I, Lourens LJ, McCarren H, Kroon D. 2005. Rapid acidification of the ocean during the Paleocene-Eocene thermal maximum. Science 308(5728): 1611-1615.

Appendix 1. Agency Programs Involved in Ocean Acidification Research

National Oceanic and Atmospheric Administration (NOAA), Department of Commerce

NOAA's mission is to understand and predict changes in Earth's environment and to conserve and manage coastal and marine resources to meet our Nation's economic, social, and environmental needs. In keeping with this mission and the requirements of the FOARAM Act, NOAA is: (1) developing and deploying enhanced ocean and coastal observing systems; (2) conducting research and developing outreach plans to ensure protection of NOAA-managed resources including fishery species and place-based protected areas; (3) developing models to forecast future ocean chemistry and impacts on fishery species; and (4) educating the general public. As required by the FOARAM Act, NOAA has established a NOAA Ocean Acidification Program Office. The office is responsible for coordination of ocean acidification activities across NOAA and will serve a coordinating role for NOAA Ocean Acidification activities as related to other Federal agencies, international inquiries, the media, Congress, non-governmental organizations, and the general public.

Scientists from **NOAA's Office of Oceanic and Atmospheric Research** work collaboratively with academic partners to conduct ocean carbon cycle research from ships, moorings, and floats in all major ocean basins. Current programs focus on open-ocean physical and biogeochemical observations in support of long-term monitoring and prediction of the ocean environment on time scales from hours to decades. Studies are conducted to improve understanding of the complex physical and biogeochemical processes operating in the world oceans, to define the forcing functions and processes driving ocean circulation and the ocean carbon system, and to improve environmental forecasting capabilities and other supporting services for marine commerce and fisheries. Included are studies to assess the ocean's role in controlling atmospheric CO_2 levels with focus on observations of the exchange of CO_2 across the air-sea interface and its eventual penetration into the water masses of the deep ocean. Scientists within these laboratories are collaborating closely with NOAA Fisheries surveys and experimental research to assist in the analysis of carbon data samples and to expand the sampling effort related to carbon chemistry of the ocean, as it relates to managed and protected species. NOAA also plans to fund new sensor development related to detection and monitoring of ocean acidification through the Ocean Acidification Program.

NOAA National Marine Fisheries Service studies are focused on assessing the physiological effects on individual living marine resources and the resulting ecosystem impacts. Through laboratory, field, and modeling studies, potential impacts are being examined on commercially and recreationally important fish and shellfish species and other species that are important components of marine ecosystems, including protected species. As noted above, collaborations with other parts of NOAA to monitor ocean acidification are ongoing.

Within the **National Ocean Service,** NOAA is conducting estuary baseline research and plans to administrate a broader research program focused on the study of the impacts of ocean acidification on ocean and coastal ecosystems, including the development of ecosystem models to forecast future ecological, cultural, and economic impacts. In addition, a research effort to develop an ecosystem monitoring network for coral reefs is continuing. Regionally specific ocean acidification research and outreach plans to manage and protect marine sanctuaries are being developed as are plans to enhance long-term monitoring of ocean acidification-related parameters at **National Estuarine Research Reserves**. Ocean acidification-related data are also being collected and served by the **Integrated Ocean Observing System** via its regional associations.

The National Oceanographic Data Center (NODC) within **NOAA's National Environmental Satellite, Data, and Information Service (NESDIS)** serves the NOAA OAP and the broader ocean acidification community by providing dedicated online data discovery and access, long-term preservation, archival, coordinated data flow, and scientific stewardship for a diverse range of ocean acidification and other chemical, physical, and biological oceanographic data. NODC builds on a highly collaborative approach with shared responsibilities among scientists and data managers, within and external to NOAA.

Scientists in NESDIS have also advanced the development of an experimental product that tracks ocean acidification within surface waters of the greater Caribbean Region by merging ship, satellite, and synoptic model datasets. The model has been used to derive trends in ocean acidification within the region extending back more than two decades and examines seasonal dynamics, which offer insight into potential areas of refugia or increased risk to ocean acidification particularly with respect to coral reef ecosystems in the region.

Department of the Interior (DOI)

The U.S. Department of the Interior's (DOI) marine and coastal responsibilities include 84 marine and coastal National Parks and 180 National Wildlife Refuges, numerous threatened and endangered species that depend on the ocean for survival, and some marine mammals including the polar bear, walrus, manatee, and sea otter. DOI also shares a concern for preserving these ecosystems and managing natural resources within these and other areas. The Department also manages offshore energy production and must take into consideration the environmental effects of these activities in relation to other environmental stresses. Ocean acidification will alter the environment and may have serious implications for the important areas managed by DOI, particularly since these areas include diverse ecosystems, such as coral and estuarine communities, and sediment resources. An understanding of the implications of ocean acidification is necessary to better manage these areas and to provide for adaptation to the altered environment. DOI, therefore, needs to be actively participating in identifying research needs as well as ensuring that appropriate scientific information is gathered to inform decision making.

o National Park Service (NPS),

o National Park Service (NPS), The National Park Service is entrusted with managing 84 ocean and Great Lakes parks across 26 states and territories. These parks conserve over 12,500 miles of coast and 2.4 million acres of ocean and Great Lakes waters. NPS has adopted strategies to enhance the agency's organizational and scientific capacity to understand and conserve ocean and coastal park resources with state and Federal agencies and local organizations. The NPS conducts assessments of submerged maritime historic and cultural resources, and assessments of coastal watersheds and water resource conditions. The NPS also conducts long-term monitoring of marine ecosystems within its jurisdiction and maintains inventories of natural resources. The NPS Inventory and Monitoring Program provides a set of 12 baseline natural resource inventories on National Parks, which include presence, class, distribution, and status of biological resources such as plants and animals, and abiotic resources such as air, water, soils, and climate in certain coastal and estuarine locations.

o United States Geological Survey (USGS)

The USGS mission, as a bureau of DOI, is to provide sound scientific knowledge and information needed to understand environmental quality and resource preservation on regional, national, and, when appropriate, global scales. A number of programs within the USGS address such needs, including the Coastal and Marine Geology Program, Earth Surface Dynamics and Climate Change Research and Development, Core Science Systems (CSS), and various USGS Biology and Water Programs. Within the marine realm, the Coastal and Marine Geology Program and Climate Change coordinators recognize a need for research linking climate change and ocean acidification to marine ecosystem responses because of the significant resource management implications. Within the terrestrial aquatic realm, changes in river and lake chemistries have been characterized and monitored by USGS for decades. USGS research will continue to provide fundamental information on carbon and CO_2 cycling in these important areas and these data will aid the development of models that describe ecosystem responses to chemical changes in the ocean and aquatic environments. In collaboration with programs working in the marine and terrestrial realms, the CSS program facilitates the integration and application of data to understand complex earth surface processes such as ocean acidification.

o United States Fish and Wildlife Service (FWS)

The FWS has responsibility for many natural resources that could be affected by ocean acidification. The FWS Migratory Bird Program conserves migratory seabird populations and their habitats through careful monitoring, effective management, and by supporting national and international partnerships. The FWS also has legal responsibility for many marine species listed under the Endangered Species Act and Marine Mammal Protection Act. The FWS is concerned with how ocean acidification will affect the marine food webs that support these trust species. The FWS also manages the National Wildlife Refuge System, which includes 106 marine protected areas, and shares management responsibility for four large Marine National Monuments in the Pacific Ocean. The Refuge System protects the most remote and relatively pristine coral reef ecosystems under U.S. jurisdiction. These coral reef refuges serve as ideal natural laboratories for studying the effects of climate change and ocean acidification in the absence of other major human disturbances.

o Bureau of Ocean Energy and Management (BOEM)

The BOEM environmental studies group is funding ocean acidification monitoring and research in the Arctic and potentially in the Gulf of Mexico. BOEM is also leading monitoring and collection of baseline information related to oil leases in the Chukchi and Beaufort Seas.

o Other DOI agencies with missions related to ocean acidification include the Bureau of Indian Affairs (BIA) and the Bureau of Land Management (BLM).

Department of State (DOS)

The U.S. Department of State (DOS) recognizes the importance of ocean acidification and its role in addressing this issue on an international scale with the cooperation of international partners. Although it does not currently manage any dedicated programs or funds for ocean acidification, DOS, along with the U.S. Agency for International Development (USAID), is already progressing the understanding and acknowledgement of this issue. For example, DOS has raised ocean acidification in relevant international fora to advance public diplomacy, such as the Pacific Regional Environmental Programme, and has provided funding to various international ocean acidification activities, including the international workshop "Economics of Ocean Acidification". Involvement by DOS in this issue will likely increase and become more proactive, especially in the Bureau of Oceans and International Environmental and Scientific Affairs.

Environmental Protection Agency (EPA)

Under the Clean Air Act, EPA has developed regulations for the transportation and industrial sectors to reduce emissions of carbon dioxide and other greenhouse gases that contribute to ocean acidification, and EPA implements the Greenhouse Gas Reporting Program which will provide data to inform future Agency policies related to climate change. EPA is also responsible for protecting aquatic resources under the Clean Water Act, which charges EPA, States, Tribes and Territories to maintain and restore the chemical, physical, and biological integrity of the Nation's waters. The Act sets out several national goals, including the protection and propagation of fish, shellfish, and wildlife and recreation in and on the water through enforcement of physical, chemical, and biological water quality standards. EPA supports actions to improve standards and reporting for marine and estuarine pH and is developing biological water quality standards for coral reefs and other aquatic resources, which can be used to protect against the consequences of ocean acidification.

National Aeronautics and Space Administration (NASA)

NASA's Earth Science Research Program supports research activities that address the Earth system to characterize its properties, to understand the naturally occurring and human-induced processes that drive them, and to improve our capability for predicting its future evolution. The focus of the Earth Science Research Program is the use of space-based measurements to provide information not available by other means.

The goals of the NASA Earth Science Research Program for Carbon Cycle Science are to improve understanding of the global carbon cycle and to quantify changes in atmospheric CO_2 and methane concentrations as well as terrestrial and aquatic carbon storage in response to fossil fuel combustion, land use and land cover change, and other human activities and natural events. NASA carbon cycle research encompasses multiple temporal and spatial scales and addresses atmospheric, terrestrial, and aquatic carbon reservoirs, their coupling within the global carbon cycle, and interactions with climate and other aspects of the Earth system.

Past projects have supported observation, research, modeling, satellite instrument requirement development, and education and public outreach investments in ocean acidification. In the most recent Carbon Cycle Science program element, NASA encouraged proposals for studies that address our understanding of ocean acidification and the impacts and feedbacks on ocean chemistry, ecology, and biology. These included but were not limited to: (1) the impact of increasing or high CO_2 concentrations on ocean chemistry; (2) the evolving ability of the oceans to take up CO_2; and (3) the characterization and delineation of possible interactions between the effects of increasing pCO_2 and effects due to climate-induced changes in variables such as temperature and nutrients. To the extent possible, predictions of changes and quantification and characterization of impacts and feedbacks of ocean acidification on the broad ocean system, especially carbon dynamics, with the associated errors, were encouraged. Development of educational materials and outreach strategies related to ocean acidification and associated policies were also encouraged.

National Science Foundation (NSF)

The NSF supports a broad spectrum of ocean acidification-related research and educational activities that spans multiple disciplines, as well as capacity building within the scientific community.

Within the NSF's Directorate for Geosciences/Division of Ocean Sciences, Chemical and Biological Oceanography program managers have utilized funds from their core programs in the past few years to initiate ocean acidification research and technology development. The Biological Oceanography Program supports investigations of the impacts of ocean acidification on the biology, ecology, and biogeochemistry of planktonic and benthic systems of both the open ocean and coastal region, while the Chemical Oceanography Program has a strong emphasis on the impacts of ocean acidification on organic and inorganic geochemical materials in the oceans. Similar interests and investments exist in the NSF Office of Polar Programs.

Other NSF programs have also made investments in ocean acidification research. The Marine Geology and Geophysics program considers the genesis, chemistry, and mineralogical evolution of marine sediments, as well as interactions of continental and marine geologic processes and paleo-oceanography; and the Geobiology and Low-Temperature Geochemistry program promotes studies of the interactions between biological and geological systems at all space and time scales. NSF's Program on Dynamics of Coupled Natural and Human Systems contributes to advance the ability to understand and predict the cultural and economic impacts of ocean acidification.

Finally, NSF's LTER supports the type of long-term interdisciplinary research necessary to understand the consequences of ocean acidification at the ecosystem scale.

The Directorate for Geosciences, the Directorate for Biological Sciences, and the Office of Polar Programs at the NSF together manage a limited-duration, focused program on ocean acidification to support research on three main research areas: (1) the chemistry and physical chemistry of ocean acidification and, in particular, its interplay with fundamental biochemical and physiological processes of organisms; (2) how ocean acidification interacts with processes at the organismal level, and how such interactions impact the structure and function of ecosystems; and (3) how the earth system history informs our understanding of the effects of ocean acidification on the present day and future ocean.

United States Navy

The U.S. Navy concerns surrounding ocean acidification stem from its relationship to climate change and national security. The Navy's Task Force Climate Change, which is directed by the Oceanographer of the Navy, was created to address the implications of climate change for national security and naval operations to ensure that the Navy is ready and capable to meet all mission requirements in the 21st century. Ocean acidification has the potential to increase instability in regions of the world where the effects of decreasing pH on marine life will threaten the food supply of over one billion people. The Navy is currently monitoring ongoing research to assess the implications of ocean acidification on future missions.

Appendix 2. Agency Budget Estimates by Theme

The FY12 Budget below represents funds, in thousands of dollars, for the purposes of implementing Themes 1-7 of the Strategic Research Plan.

	EPA	NASA	NOAA	NSF#	USGS	TOTAL ^
FY 12 Budget Estimates (Total - All themes)*	$0	$2,025	$6,358	$13,000	$1,755	$23,138
Theme 1: Research to Understand Responses to Ocean Acidification	$0	$1,125	$1,282	$10,000	$354	**$12,761**
Theme 2: Monitoring of Ocean Chemical and Biological Impacts	$0	$375	$3,721	$1,000	$1,201	**$6,297**
Theme 3: Modeling to Predict Changes in the Ocean Carbon Cycle and Impacts on Marine Ecosystems and Organisms	$0	$375	$654	$1,000	$100	**$2,129**
Theme 4: Technology Development and Standardization of Measurements	$0	$0	$287	$300	$25	**$612**
Theme 5: Assessment of Socioeconomic Impacts and Development of Strategies to Conserve Marine Organisms and Ecosystems	$0	$0	$92	$0	$0	**$92**
Theme 6: Education, Outreach, and Engagement Strategy on Ocean Acidification	$0	$150	$132	$500	$25	**$807**
Theme 7: Data Management and Integration	$0	$0	$190	$200	$50	**$440**

*Agency totals are based upon the FY 2012 Budget. Allocation among the themes is estimated.

Costs for the NOAA OA Program Office, including 3 full-time employees, will come out of this budget, assuming no other funds are designated for this purpose.

^ Other Federal agencies not included here may have indirect activities that could be enhanced or modified to address ocean acidification.

Appendix 3. Acronyms and Abbreviations

AAAS	American Association for the Advancement of Science
AGU	American Geophysical Union
AOAT	Atlantic Ocean Acidification Test-Bed
ASLO	American Society of Limnology and Oceanography
ARMS	Autonomous Reef Monitoring Structures
ASTC	Association of Science - Technology Centers
AUVs	Autonomous underwater vehicles
BCO-DMO	Biological and Chemical Oceanography Data Management Office
BOEM	Bureau of Ocean Energy Management
BOGCM	Biogeochemistry ocean general circulation model
$CaCO_3$	Calcium carbonate
CCEP	Climate Change Education Partnership
CLEAN	Climate Literacy and Energy Awareness Network
CLIVAR	Climate Variability and Predictability Program
CMIP5	Coupled Model Intercomparison Project, Phase 5
CO_2	Carbon dioxide
CO_3	Carbonate
CoML	Census of Marine Life
COSEE	Centers for Ocean Sciences Education Excellence, NSF
CRCP	Coral Reef Conservation Program
CRED	Coral Reef Ecosystem Division (NOAA Pacific Islands Fisheries Science Center)
CRMs	Certified Reference Materials
DIC	Dissolved inorganic carbon

DMAC	Data Management and Communications
DOC	Dissolved organic carbon
DOE	Department of Energy
DOI	Department of the Interior
DOM	Dissolved organic matter
DOS	Department of State
EPA	Environmental Protection Agency
EPOCA	European Project on Ocean Acidification
FOARAM Act	Federal Ocean Acidification Research and Monitoring Act of 2009
FOCE	Free-ocean carbon dioxide enrichment experiment
FWS	U.S. Fish and Wildlife Service
GEO-IDE	Global Earth Observation-Integrated Data Environment
GEOSS	Global Earth Observation System of Systems
IAEA	International Atomic Energy Agency
IAM	Integrated Assessment Models
IMBER	Integrated Marine Biogeochemistry and Ecosystem Research
IOOS	Integrated Ocean Observing System
IPCC	Intergovernmental Panel on Climate Change
IWG-OA	Interagency Working Group on Ocean Acidification
I&M	Inventory and Monitoring
JPL	Jet Propulsion Laboratory
LCC	Landscape Conservation Cooperatives
LTER	Long-term Ecological Research (Network)
MPA	Marine Protected Areas
NASA	National Aeronautics and Space Administration
NEP	National Estuary Program
NERRS	National Estuarine Research Reserve System

NGO	Non-governmental organization
NOAA	National Oceanic and Atmospheric Administration
NODC	National Oceanographic Data Center
NOC	National Ocean Council
NRC	National Research Council
NPS	National Park Service
NRInfo	Natural Resource Information Portal
NSF	National Science Foundation
NWRS	National Wildlife Refuge System
OA-ISMAs	Ocean acidification intensively studied marine areas
OATF	Ocean Acidification Task Force
OCB	Ocean Carbon and Biogeochemistry (Program)
ORRAP	Ocean Research and Resources Advisory Panel
OPTF	Ocean Policy Task Force
OSSEs	Observing System Simulation Experiments
pCO_2	Partial pressure of carbon dioxide
PICCC	Pacific Islands Climate Change Cooperative
PIC	Particulate inorganic carbon
PIFSC	Pacific Islands Fisheries Science Center
POC	Particulate organic carbon
QA/QC	Quality assurance/quality control
ROMS	Regional Ocean Modeling Systems
SCC	Social Cost of Carbon
SeaBASS	SeaWiFS (Sea-viewing Wide Field-of-view Sensor) Bio-optical Archive and Storage System
SEES	Science, Engineering and Education for Sustainability
SHARQ	Submersible Habitat for Analyzing Reef Quality

SOCAT   Surface Ocean Carbon Atlas

SOLAS   Surface Ocean Lower Atmosphere Study

SOPs   Standard Operating Procedures

SOST   Subcommittee on Ocean Science and Technology

TA   Total alkalinity

USGS   U.S. Geological Survey

USDA   United States Department of Agriculture

USGCRP   U.S. Global Change Research Program

VOS   Voluntary Observing Ships

WCRP   World Climate Research Program

Appendix 4. Informational Websites

National Ocean Policy Implementation Plan	http://www.whitehouse.gov/administration/eop/oceans/policy
Responses to EPA Notice of Data Availability From Ocean Carbon and Biogeochemistry Program	www.us-ocb.org/publications/EPA_OCB_FINAL.pdf
Great Lakes Monitoring	www.epa.gov/glnpo/monitoring/guard/ship.html
Argo	www.argo.ucsd.edu
FOCE Development	www.mbari.org/highCO2 /foce/home.htm
Long Term Ecological Research Network	www.lternet.edu/
The Global Ocean Ship-based Hydrographic Investigations Program	www.go-ship.org/HydroMan.html
PMEL Coral Reef Moorings	www.pmel.noaa.gov/CO2 /story/Coral+Reef+Moorings
Census of Coral Reef Ecosystems	www.creefs.org/about.html
HAB Prevention, Control and Mitigation (PCM)	www.cop.noaa.gov/stressors/extremeevents/hab/current/PCM_08.aspx
Alliance for Coastal Technologies	www.act-us.info/rft.php
Social Cost of Carbon for Regulatory Impact Analysis	www.epa.gov/oms/climate/regulations/scc-tsd.pdf
Landscape Conservation Cooperative	www.fws.gov/science/shc/lcc.html
Pacific Islands Climate Change Cooperative	http://hawaiiconservation.org/activities/pacific_island_climate_change_cooperative
Ocean Margin Ecosystems Group for Acidification Studies	omegas.science.oregonstate.edu/
Ocean Ark Alliance	www.oceanacidification.net
Understanding Ocean Acidification	www.cisanctuary.org/acidocean/
PMEL Carbon Program	www.pmel.noaa.gov/CO2/
Ocean Carbon & Biogeochemistry	www.us-ocb.org
European Project on Ocean Acidification	www.epoca-project.eu
Integrated Marine Biogeochemistry and Ecosystem Research	http://www.imber.info/
Education Resources - Climate	www.education.noaa.gov/Climate/
Centers for Ocean Sciences Education Excellence	www.cosee.net/
Students Guide to Global Climate Change	www.epa.gov/climatechange/kids/index.htm
Integrated Ocean Observing System	www.ioos.gov/data/welcome.html
NOAA National Oceanographic Data Center	www.nodc.noaa.gov/oceanacidification/
Biological and Chemical Oceanography Data Management Office	www.bco-dmo.org/
Ocean Observatories Initiative	www.ci.oceanobservatories.org
Earth Cube	www.nsf.gov/geo/earthcube/
SeaBass	www.seabass.gsfc.nasa.gov/

Integrated Resource Management Applications	https://nrinfo.nps.gov/
Water Quality Web Services	www.qwwebservices.usgs.gov/
The National Map	www.nationalmap.gov/
Science Base	www.sciencebase.gov/
Ocean Biogeographic Information System	www.usgs.gov/obis-usa/
Carbon Dioxide Information Analysis Center	www.cdiac.ornl.gov/
Ontology Registry and Repository	www.mmisw.org/orr/#http://mmisw.org/ont/ioos/OA
Surface Ocean CO2 Atlas	www.socat.info/
Program for Climate Model Diagnosis and Inter-comparison	www-pcmdi.llnl.gov/

Appendix 5. Glossary

Acclimate – refers to phenotypic changes during an organism's lifetime in response to environmental changes.

Adaptation (Climate Change) – adjustment in natural or human systems in response to actual or expected climatic stimuli or their effects, which moderates harm or exploits beneficial opportunities.

Adaptation (Biological) – the process or the product of natural selection that changes the behavior, function, or structure of an organism physiological function or an anatomical structure of an organism that better suit it to its environment.

Adaptive Capacity – the ability of a species to become adapted (i.e., to be able to live and reproduce) to a certain range of environmental conditions as a result of genetic and phenotypic responses.

Anthropogenic – of, relating to, or resulting from the influence of human beings on nature.

Biodiversity – the variability among living organisms from all sources including terrestrial, marine, and other aquatic ecosystems and the ecological complexes of which they are part; this includes diversity within species, among species, and of ecosystems.

Climate Change – a significant and lasting change in the statistical distribution of weather patterns over periods ranging from decades to millions of years. It may be a change in average weather conditions or the distribution of events around that average (e.g., more or fewer extreme weather events). Climate change may be limited to a specific region or may occur across the whole Earth.

Climate Modeling – quantitative methods to simulate the interactions of the atmosphere, oceans, land surface, and ice. They are used for a variety of purposes from study of the dynamics of the climate system to projections of future climate.

Downscaling – refers to techniques that take output from the model and add information at scales smaller than the grid spacing. Downscaling methods are developed to obtain local-scale surface weather from regional-scale atmospheric variables.

Ecosystem – a biological environment consisting of all the organisms living in a particular area, as well as all the nonliving (abiotic), physical components of the environment with which the organisms interact.

Ecosystem Services – the benefits people obtain from ecosystems. These include provisioning services such as food and water; regulation services such as the regulation of climate, floods, disease, wastes, and water quality; cultural services such as recreation, aesthetic enjoyment, and spiritual fulfillment; and supporting services such as photosynthesis and nutrient cycling.

Eutrophication – the movement of a body of water's trophic status in the direction of increasing biomass, by the addition of artificial or natural substances, such as nitrates and phosphates, through fertilizers or sewage, to an aquatic system.

Habitat – an ecological or environmental area that is inhabited by a particular species of animal, plant, or other type of organism. It is the natural environment in which an organism lives, or the physical environment that surrounds (influences and is utilized by) a species population.

Harmful Algal Blooms – a rapid increase or accumulation in the population of algae in an aquatic system forming visible patches that may harm the health of the environment, plants, or animals. They can deplete the oxygen and block the sunlight that other organisms need to live, and some algae blooms release toxins that are dangerous to animals and humans.

Hydrogen Ion Concentration – the hydrogen ion concentration in seawater is reported as pH = -log10[H+]

Hydrology – the movement, distribution, and quality of water, including the hydrologic cycle, water resources, and environmental watershed sustainability.

Hypoxia – a phenomenon that occurs in aquatic environments as dissolved oxygen becomes reduced in concentration to a point where it becomes detrimental to aquatic organisms living in the system.

Indicator Species – A species whose presence, absence, or relative well-being in a given environment is a sign of the overall health of its ecosystem. By monitoring the condition and behavior of an indicator species, scientists can determine how changes in the environment and likely to affect other species that are more difficult to study.

Mitigation – in the context of climate change, a human intervention to reduce the sources or enhance the sinks of greenhouse gases.

Ocean Acidification – the ongoing decrease in the pH and increase in acidity of the Earth's oceans, caused by the uptake of carbon dioxide from the atmosphere.

Resilience – the capacity of an ecosystem to return to the pre-condition state following a perturbation, including maintaining its essential characteristics taxonomic composition, structures, ecosystem functions, and process rates.

Socioeconomics – a word used to identify the importance of factors other than biology in natural resource management decisions. For example, if management results in more fishing income, it is important to know how the income is distributed between small and large boats or part-time and full-time fishermen.

Stakeholders – a person, group, organization, or system that affects or can be affected by an organization's actions.

Total Alkalinity – the total alkalinity of a sea water sample is defined as the number of moles of hydrogen ion equivalent to the excess of proton acceptors (bases formed from weak acids with a dissociation constant $K \leq 10\text{-}4.5$ at 25°C and zero ionic strength) over proton donors (acids with $K \geq 10\text{-}4.5$) in 1 kilogram of sample.